BEYOND THE MUSIC:

AN INTRODUCTION TO THE MUSIC INDUSTRY

By Rick DiGiallonardo and John Fishell

Ball State University

cognella™
San Diego, CA

Bassim Hamadeh, Publisher
Michael Simpson, Vice President of Acquisitions
Christopher Foster, Vice President of Marketing
Jessica Knott, Managing Editor
Stephen Milano, Creative Director
Kevin Fahey, Cognella Marketing Program Manager
Al Grisanti, Acquisitions Editor
Jamie Giganti, Project Editor
Brian Fahey, Licensing Associate

First published in the United States of America in 2012 by University Readers, Inc.

16 15 14 13 12   1 2 3 4 5

Printed in the United States of America

ISBN: 978-1-60927-738-3

www.cognella.com 800.200.3908

CONTENTS

Throughout this book you will find markers like the one you see below. These sections are included in your text for you to write notes on your own thoughts or special points to remember about what you've read, ideas concerning the topic, etc. When a companion webpage is setup, I look forward to reading those sections and adding your input to the next edition!

CHAPTER 1

Finding the Record Deal

The elusive record deal or record contract is the so-called Golden Ring that all bands, solo artists, artist managers, and more seek. The idea of acquiring a recording contract with a major record label arouses emotions of big houses, fast cars, piles of cash, thousands of fans screaming your name, traveling the world. The reality in today's music industry is that nothing could be further from the truth. Now, don't get me wrong. Are there artists in the industry today who have everything mentioned above and more? Sure ... there's Lady Gaga, Jay-Z, Beyoncé, My Chemical Romance, Kings of Leon, and others. HOWEVER, these are the exceptions to the rule. Why would I say this, when the majority of all acts that are signed to major or indie labels go through the process of recording the album, mixing, mastering, and duplication. When all of that is complete, the record company will send out what are known as free goods, which is copies of your CD to the MD (music director), PD (program director), or DJ (disc jockey) in the hopes of getting them to spin a particular song from the CD. What happens is that most of CDs sent out do not get radio play. And, without radio play, your career with that label is over. Let me explain.

Let's start from the beginning, shall we? First, know that an entire book can be and has been written on this very topic. So, we'll approach this by giving you the main points. We will assume that at this point in your music career you and your musical companions have been playing in clubs for at least two years, and every now and then, open for a signed act at a fair, music festival, or even a large venue. Your fan base has been steadily growing; established and new fans visit the band's Webpage to find out where you'll be performing next, what new adventures the band has experienced, and just to ogle certain band members they are infatuated with. As well as having your fan base locked and loaded, entertainment venues are now calling you, instead of the other way around, to request dates for the band to perform at their establishment. Also, you and a couple of the other band members have been writing new material for the band to perform ... so it's time to book time in a recording studio to record a full CD to complement the EP you recorded and released on your own a while ago. Things are looking bright and headed in the right direction. You're feeling that it's time to make the move and shoot for the elusive record deal. Fortunately, you hired a personal manager for the band about a year ago who intimately knows all the good and the bad about the band, and what's more, they know how to properly market you to the labels. (More on that in the chapter about Artist

Managers.) The leader of the band and main songwriter or songwriters attend a meeting to discuss shopping for a label deal. Unfortunately, the individuals just mentioned, at least in the industry's opinion, are the most important entities of the band and the rest of you are ... I hate to say, expendable. And, since the labels have the most say as to what will or will not happen concerning the band's future, this is something you'll just have to come to grips with and hope for the best that you're not replaced by some hot studio player. Back to the manager. After discussing the past year's events, the band and the manager assess the band's progress and determine if it's time to approach a label for a deal. REMEMBER ... first impressions are lasting and that impression will be the one that the record companies will remember. So, do not approach a label until you are certain you're prepared and ready to compete on a national and international level!

Thus far I've brought you up to the point of the manager picking up the phone to begin setting up appointments with various record labels to shop the band. This is how it used to be, and for the most part, still is. However, things are changing at such a rapid pace in the industry that bands, managers, and the labels must adapt to the ever-changing technology that allows the bands and the labels to shop deals in a different manner. Now, we put everything on our band Webpage, including QuickTime movies of live performances, still shots, MP3 samples of the old and new music the band has written, and more. All the label has to do is pull up the site on the computer and see if you are something they are interested in, and that you might be the next big thing to hit in the industry.

One important point to always consider is if your music is too eclectic, new, or different, you won't get the deal. If it's too much like someone they already have signed to the label or who is on the radio, you won't get the deal. The key is to find the fine line, the middle ground that shows you are unique, yet have familiar qualities that fans can relate to and will encourage them to purchase your CD, and buy tickets to see you perform live in concert.

Ok, we're almost ready, so whom do we contact now? If you are a band with no management, DO NOT CONTACT ANYONE. A band should never represent themselves, ever! This can be and usually is the kiss of death for your career. Either the band's personal manager, entertainment attorney, or both should do the negotiations on your behalf. Your job is to create music, not broker record deals. Usually by this time, the labels already know something about you from your regional success and sales of your self-produced CDs. The individual your manager will most likely deal with at the label is the A&R person. A&R stands for Artist and Repertoire. This individual has permission from the CEO of the labels to find, negotiate, and sign new artists. A&R representatives, with most labels, have experience in the genre, sales, marketing, and promotion concerning your kind of band and your music. I've met A&R representatives who have "no" musical knowledge whatsoever. They couldn't tell you the difference between a C-major chord and a Chevy Blazer. But, they do have an ear as to what sounds good in relation to what the public would want to hear, they know what sells—and more, what does not sell—in the music industry, which is the bottom line for most labels, so give them the respect they deserve, as they are generally the main contact between you and the bigwigs at the label. The A&R person should be very positive about you, your songs, stage presence, everything. Why? Because they wouldn't be searching you out if they didn't have an interest in signing you. As stated, the industry is in such a state of flux that if an A&R representative from a label contacts you, it's most likely to broker a deal.

WHO'S REALLY IN CHARGE

Let me pause here and present you with a list of the major players at a record company. Record companies generally follow the typical business structure. There is the CEO/President, generally the owner of the company; the Vice-President or Vice-Presidents; then would come your A&R, Artist and Repertoire people. There are generally many A&R individuals at a label, one for each major genre of music: Rock, Pop, Alternative, Hip-Hop, Rap, and so forth. There are labels that have gifted individuals who know several genres of music; these individuals could be managing more than one music genre/area. Once the individuals above decide on a band they would like to sign, they will work hand in hand with the Sales and Marketing departments. These are the people who put your product out in stores for purchase. Then there is the Promotion department. Depending on the label, these people can serve many purposes in promoting the music; however, their main job is to try to get your music played on the radio. Then there's the Business and Legal departments, which are responsible for the contracts signed by bands, legal advice on copyright, licensing, and the like. The Business department will also be involved in the development of a record deal along with Legal and A&R, as well as decide what the label should pay for and what not to pay for in contracts, promotion, etc. Production/Product Management will make certain the product is on time in relation to release dates, Artwork, Sales, etc. They are the gatekeepers of the departments that turn the recording or master into a viable, selling product. Distribution handles the dissemination of the product to the masses, meaning they get the product into the right hands in order to sell mass units. Marketing will handle items such as advertising, music videos, promotional materials, and much more to enhance sales. The Publicity department will make certain the "right" information, be it true or make believe, is published in the trades, put on television and radio, etc. They are the people who make you the artists they need you to be as far as how they want the record-buying public to perceive you. Finance, as in any company, tracks the money and distributes income to the correct individuals. There are other minor departments that work hand in hand with the departments mentioned.

Digital/New Media. Time to bring your product into the twenty-first century. This area will handle everything from digital downloads and the digital delivery of your product through companies such as Apple's iTunes, Rhapsody, Netflix, and many more.

Lastly, some labels have an International department, which will handle items when your music reaches other countries. Most of the time a label will work in conjunction with another label that has established connections and businesses set up in other countries, and your label will work with them in the distribution of your music in the countries those labels represent.

NEGOTIATING THE DEAL (and important facts behind the deal)

Okay, now that we've discussed the basics of the major areas within a label, let's get back to talking about how we land a deal for you and your band. Probably the best way to attract a label's attention is described in two sections. First, you must be writing and performing original music. No copy band in the world gets signed to a label, with maybe the exception of Weird Al Yankovic, who writes great parodies based on major hits from other artists. But, if he does a song you've written … you must be a success! Your original music must be fresh, exciting, new, and relatable. Write music that the audience finds familiar. Any time you can tap into the listener's ear or mind and capture them with a musical theme within the lyrics, or a familiar beat or sound, you'll be on your way to selling some recordings.

Many bands have asked, "How many original songs do we need to have before approaching a label?" Well, let me put it this way … the label probably won't like ninety percent of what you play and what's worse, they will state that they don't hear the "hit" potential of the song. What does this mean for your band's writers? Plain and simple … have at least 200 songs in the can. I know, most of you are thinking, "this guy is nuts! That's a ton of songs!" Believe me, you'll need them. Most songwriters always think the last song they wrote is their best. However, there might be a song in your repertoire from days gone by that with some simple arrangement changes can be made into a hit. Another very important part of your songwriting is that you should be writing music every day! Not every other day or when "inspiration strikes"—write music every day! Why? It's your job! The more you write, the more you'll have to present to the record company to choose from. The more songs you have, the stronger your message to the label that you are a prolific writer and that you'll have plenty of material for more albums, which every label wants and needs. Some labels have what are known as in-house writers, much like the publishing companies had in the early 1920s and 1930s. These music-writing machines generally work for the label's in-house publishing company and can write you a song for your upcoming CD. This means rather than getting the full royalties, you'll be splitting them with the rights holder, whether that's the writer or the record company. So, a word to the wise: Write, write, write!

Secondly, you should be at least a regional success as a performing band. Many can and have come up with what they think is a successful performing act. For us, let's say this means that within a four-state region of where your band is based, every club/venue where your band performs is always filled with your fans. HINT: These fans will buy your CDs that you sell at your shows. Now, if you are playing four nights per week and selling CDs at every show, you'll soon sell thousands of units. If you are selling that many units, some radio station in one of the cities you are performing in will most likely spin your CD … with the proper persuasion by your management, and other added incentives. Bottom line is if you can sell at least 10,000 units (CDs) on your own, imagine what the majors can do for you with their monster-marketing machine and contacts behind them. And, they know this! If you can sell 10,000 units on your own, chances are it's quite possible that a major record label can sell 500,000 units, if not more.

Selling 500,000 or more units is designated as "Gold" sales/status in the U.S. Selling 1,000,000 units or more in the U.S. is designated as "Platinum" sales/status. In today's music industry, sales of that quantity will ensure your career is on its way! We haven't even discussed the sales of digital downloads of singles or CDs, audio streaming, and other activities.

I know that I'm focusing primarily on the major record labels at this time. The same principles apply to the Indie record labels as well, which will be addressed later in the book. Statistically the numbers of sales are generally not as large as they are with a major label because of its much smaller operating budget and not having near the massive distribution power the major labels operate within.

Now you think you're ready for a deal. The A&R representative has been in contact with your personal manager, they've flown out to speak with you and your management, and they've seen your show. Your band's been given the supreme L.A. schmooze routine, and now you're fired up to sign on the dotted line. But wait … there's something in the back of your mind telling you, or I hope there is …"Are you certain this is the right record company for you and your band?"

If that is one of your thoughts, congratulations, you are right on the mark to a future in the industry. You must be certain the A&R person you've been negotiating with has a strong belief in you and your music—as much as, if not more than you and your manager have. This is imperative, as the A&R is your lifeline to the label.

When you are negotiating any deal, find out as much as you can about the person who will be representing you as they are trying to find out about you and your band. What kind of music do they listen to? Have they ever signed any other acts that are like yours? How successful have those acts become? After you've gotten all of the information you can from the A&R person, contact the management, and if possible, the bands themselves that that particular A&R representative has worked with, and ask how things have been going with the label, how responsive the label is to any requests made by the band, and if any unresolvable issues ever pop up. What happened? How did the label/A&R representative resolve those issues? Before you sign, you'll have your manager, and most certainly, an entertainment attorney read "every word" on the record contract. More on that in just a little bit.

What if everything we've discussed has been accomplished on your end? You're a regional success; you have many original songs, and are writing every day; you are constantly recording your live shows and reviewing them in order to improve the live show, lighting, costuming, and more. You're packing them in at every gig you perform, and the fans love you! Yet, the record deal still eludes you. How long do you keep up with the game before you call it quits? How long do you play the smoke-filled clubs, sometimes dealing with disreputable venue managers/owners, and others? Band members are becoming frustrated, even though your success seems steady. Your desire to write new songs wanes. What to do?

When neither you nor your management can attract the attention of the majors, it's time to bring in the heavy hitters: The entertainment attorneys.

It is a fact that the entertainment attorney is probably the best solution to getting the attention of a major label and possibly acquiring a record deal. Why? Entertainment attorneys are always in the mix, day in and day out, of the happenings within the industry. They know what new artists are being considered; they know who is getting signed, and who is getting dropped. They know what administrative changes are occurring within a record label, and all of the other intricacies within the industry.

How do they know this? That's what they do! An entertainment attorney can open doors for artist managers and their acts that the manager could never open on their own. Entertainment attorneys are constantly in contact with various labels, their artists, and the business and legal departments within the record companies. And yes, they too listen to music and sometimes find acts that they know will break, and will introduce the act to the proper individuals at specific record companies. Practically speaking, they can guide the industry in certain directions concerning genre and artist's success. And, considering the plight in which the music industry finds itself today, concerning peer-to-peer sharing, DRM, digital streaming, Intellectual Property ownership, etc.; you want, no, "must" have an entertainment attorney on your team prior to negotiating a record deal.

When you have entertainment attorneys such as Donald Passman, John Mason, Jim Zumwalt, Gregory Victoroff, E. Scott Johnson, Stephen Raucher, and many others in the industry working multi-million-dollar deals for some of the biggest artists on the planet, you must work with an entertainment attorney. I always tell my students, "You don't go to the person flipping burgers at your local burger joint and ask them how to become a millionaire; you go to a millionaire and ask them!" So don't make the foolish assumption that you, your manager, a family member, or a friend will have the answers to your questions concerning the music industry. It will be the biggest and certainly the last mistake you'll ever make in the industry. You don't have to hire a six- or seven-figure attorney to assist you, but hire a very competent entertainment attorney who has experience dealing with the label you are negotiating with and ample knowledge concerning the current music industry standards for royalties. Notice how many times I've used the word "Entertainment" attorney? Don't make another fatal mistake and hire Uncle Paul, the real estate attorney, to negotiate a record deal/contract. If you do, the only thing you'll need Uncle Paul for is finding you a very small apartment to live in when you lose everything you've worked all these years for. (Sorry if any of you actually have an Uncle Paul who's a real estate attorney. This is just an example.)

Remember, my fellow musicians, that the competition out there is fierce! There are thousands of bands and solo artists trying to achieve the same goals as you. What are you going to do to differentiate yourself from them so "you" are the one who gets the deal, or at least a potential record deal? If you want to keep your sanity, then one thing to keep in mind is "Don't compare yourself or your band with the bands in the area where you perform." That is not your competition. Don't compare yourself or your band with successful regional bands. They are not your competition. Some of you may be thinking to yourselves, "Yes they are! They are the ones we are competing against for the gig." My friend, when it comes to getting a record deal, your competition is everyone on the radio, television, the Internet, and most importantly ... charting on Billboard! They are your competition! Strive to be as good as the artist who's on the radio and performing major tours. If you perform Country music, your competition is Carrie Underwood, Rascal Flatts, Keith Urban, and others. If you're a Rock or Alternative musician, your competition includes the Kings of Leon, The Killers, and Green Day. If your musical style is Pop/Rock, then your competition is My Chemical Romance, Lady Gaga, and the list goes on. Be prepared to compete with them, and you'll have the right mindset and discipline to succeed in the industry.

Okay, I certainly hope that you're not discouraged, but encouraged by some of the information that you've read thus far. My goal is to help you, to guide you, and to give you information that most bands don't have access to or don't take the time to find out, and they suffer the consequences in the long run.

As you've been reading this chapter, we'll say that you've already accomplished all of the above. So far we've discussed finding the right record company, what major record companies do regarding signing a new act, the basic recording-company professional structure, and who the integral individuals at the record company are with whom you and your management team will be dealing. What I mean by management team is your personal manager and the entertainment attorney you decided to have help you negotiate your record contract. If everything falls into place, if you have the right sound and look, and the timing is right, chances are good that you can acquire some type of record deal. We're going to assume that that deal has now been acquired—what happens now? The multiplicity of items inclusive in a record contract is mind-boggling! Again, I stress the need for a competent entertainment attorney. Your manager, key band members who are generally the songwriter or writers, the lead singer, and the entertainment attorney will begin negotiations with the record company regarding many items. Some of these items include length of contract, advance, tour and video support, number of albums to be recorded, and other legal matters. Let's take a look at these items individually.

SHOW ME THE MONEY

Not too long ago record companies would sign an artist based on the number of albums to be recorded for the company. Depending on how prolific your songwriter or songwriters are, this amount of time could be indefinite, especially if your band owes the record company money from the advance, tour or video support, or what have you. Also, if you are one of the few bands that are very successful in their recording career, you and a few other acts signed to the record label could be floating the entire record company financially, while the majority of the other acts signed with the label are basically tax write-offs because their sales don't earn the label enough money to pay off their advance and other expenses. Because of these items and a few other incidents that have occurred in the record industry in the past fifteen years, many high-profile musicians and bands petitioned the U.S. Senate to pass a law that record companies could sign artists or bands for a maximum of seven years. This is a definite advantage for the band. However, if you're doing very well and have a great relationship with your record company, you could always extend your contract with them indefinitely. I will discuss more on the Senate hearings in the upcoming chapters.

So what is in an advance? An advance is an amount of money that the record company prepays the band for the delivery of a recorded CD, or it could be a pre-payment of royalties, or a lump sum of money that is paid for recording and production costs. Generally, the advance is paid to the band after the signing of the record contract. In today's economy, many record companies have reduced the amount of money that they will advance, particularly for a newly signed act. However we've all heard of massive amounts of money paid in an advance for well-known and established artists such as Madonna, Janet Jackson, Paul McCartney, and others. It is generally known that the advance is non-recoupable by the record company. This means that if the band does not sell a prescribed number of albums in order to recoup the advance and other funds given to them, the record company will write off the shortfall. This is a not position you want to put yourself or your band in, because if this does occur, it's very likely that the record company will release you from the contract. Advances can include things such as the cost of recording as well as the cost of the record producer, rental of musical equipment and other items to record this CD, and other costs related to the band's first recording. An advance can also be used for the shooting of a music video; however, the amount paid is generally half of the expense of the music video. Now even though I've stated that an advance is non-recoupable by the record company, it is well known that the record company always gets every penny it puts into an act. Advances or other monies are deducted from the sales of the albums. An unfortunate reality within the music industry is that many acts will receive an advance, pay off some of the expenses they owe their personal manager, and divide the rest among the band members and spend foolishly ... on a variety of items that we need not list. This is an irresponsible thing for the band to do; the advance should be used for recording and production costs, or to pay off previous debts that the band has acquired from recordings made prior to getting the record deal. If an advance is substantial, the band may not use the full amount for recording and production costs—if this is the case, then the remainder of the funds will be distributed to the artist or the band according to their internal agreement.

This concept is well illustrated in Donald Passman's book, *All You Need to Know About the Music Business*, in which he states "the record company pays a sum of money to the artist and then keeps the artist's royalties until the record company gets its money back." So if the company gives an artist $10,000 to sign a record deal, the company keeps the first $10,000 of the artist's royalties that would otherwise be payable. The process of keeping the money to recover an advance is called recoupment, and they say an advance is recoupable from royalties. Many of you after reading that statement might be thinking, "That's a rip-off!"

Let me put this in perspective for you. The record companies take a huge risk and make a large investment in the hopes that the artist they have signed is going to be successful and make money, not only for the record company, but for the artist as well. This is why I think that even though currently the music industry is in a state of flux, the record companies aren't going anywhere. They've been in the system too long, they know the system too well, and they have most, if not all, of the connections within the music industry; therefore, for taking a risk on signing a new artist, they should be compensated in some fashion. Are there record companies that have taken advantage of this particular area of signing record contracts? Of course, but the word eventually gets out and artists, their managers, and entertainment attorneys will steer clear of these particular companies.

So when discussing the terms of a contract in regards to recoupment, what exactly falls under that category? In other words, what monies can the record companies get back, or better yet, take back? The simple answer to this is almost everything. We talked about recording costs; those are recoupable via the artist's royalties. If you want to bring in a hot studio player or singer for your recording, that is recoupable by the record company. If you, the artist, or your manager should want special artwork for the CD cover, that is recoupable by the record company via the artist's royalties. In other words, be very careful, practical, and use common sense when it comes to the amount of money that you and your management decide to spend on your first recording, because it's very easy to get caught up in all the glitter and glamour that the record companies and the music industry have to offer. And for a first-timer in the industry, well, all I can say is that probably the only money that you'll be making will be from ticket sales from the gigs that you play on tour, and we certainly don't want that to happen.

The minutiae that exist within the music industry and particularly for record companies are immense. There are dozens and dozens of intricacies that are woven into the record contract and written in legalese that without an entertainment attorney, the average musician and artist manager would be lost. It's a complex subject wherein the inner workings of a record deal can vary widely from one contract to another. However, there are certain concepts and aspects of a record deal that are universal. In today's recording industry, the most-discussed topic is the ownership of intellectual property. Basically, what this means is whatever you have to do, whatever it costs you monetarily, try to maintain the ownership of the songs that you've written. The reality of the record contract 20 to 30 years ago is the same reality today wherein the record company has an enormous advantage in the way it writes the contract to protect itself. We use to say that the first two pages of a record contract states what the artist will make, and the next 88 pages state how the record company can take it all away from you. Honestly, this is in no way to demean or disparage the record companies. It's a fact that they have the advantage over the artist when it comes to contractual negotiations.

A band is offered a deal with a record company for certain number of CDs to be recorded, over a certain period of time, for a certain amount of money, which might include extras such as a signing bonus, tour support, and other amenities thrown into the mix. So are there certain rights that the artists have to protect themselves, and are there rights that the record company has to protect itself? The answer is yes to both. Some of the rights for the recording artist are as follows:

- The artist has the right to a professionally recorded CD
- The artist has the right to examine the accounting records concerning the artist or band
- The artist has a say as to who would produce the CD. (An artist needs to be very careful when they take part in the decision-making concerning who the record producer will be, where the CD will be recorded, placement of songs, etc. The reason I mention this is that when the artist takes a proactive role in deciding what will or will not happen concerning their recording, if the recording is a failure, all fingers will point to them. If you are a brand-new act with a newly signed record deal, it is best to let the record company executives and other individuals within the company make the decisions themselves with some input by the artist and their manager.)

One important item that the artist needs to remember is that they do not own their recordings, and generally have little, if any, legal say concerning what a record company does with their intellectual property. In other words, the record company has the right to do with the recording practically anything they wish, which includes not releasing the CD at all, and even assigning the rights of the intellectual property to another company.

The rights that the record company has written into the recording contract for the record deal are staggering. Remember, the record companies that have been in business for decades know every loophole possible, and the newer ones learn from the successes of their forebears. They can, and most of the time will, incorporate those loopholes into the record contract. One of the most important items to watch out for in a record contract is known as cross-collateralization. I will discuss this in detail the next chapter.

The most important thing to remember is that if you are blessed with the opportunity of being offered a record deal, do not be foolish and become overwhelmed by the amount of money that is discussed, promised, and even annotated in a record contract. The key to success in the music industry is not obtaining a large amount of money as an advance. The key is longevity! Do not forget that longevity is the key to ultimate success in the music industry.

As you can see, there are a number of items that need to be handled properly by the right professional entities within the music industry in order to acquire a record deal. In the fragile economic market that we're in today, the chances of even a very, very good band acquiring a record deal is unfortunately slim. I would like to tell you differently, but these are the facts in today's music industry. In 2010, gross receipts for concerts were down 26.6%, attendance at live concerts was down 24.4%, and the number of shows performed in 2010 was down 16%. This is not to say that there weren't any acts out there making some major coin in the live-performance arena. As a matter of fact, if your genre is hip-hop, rap, and some R&B styles, the best way to make a good living is to perform live. The unfortunate reality is that record deals negotiated for these particular genres are primarily in the record company's favor and not in the artist's favor. Again, it is not my attempt to demean or disparage the recording industry. I was extremely fortunate as an artist to be signed to a major label for years, and tour all over the world. This would have never happened had it not been for the major labels. But, that was then, and this is now ... the industry is a different beast from what it was 20 to 25 years ago. Entire textbooks have been written primarily on the topic of how to acquire a record deal. What I'm trying to do in this text is to give you an introduction to the music industry as a primer, as a preparation, to excite you, to open your mind to other questions and avenues that you would not have otherwise investigated. That being said, I'd like to go back to the very beginning of this particular chapter and add one very important item that we have not yet discussed. That item is the music itself.

You can have some smoking hot players in your band, a monster guitarist who can play just like Steve Vai; a keyboardist who can lay it down like George Duke; a drummer as diverse as a Vinnie Colaiuta; and the lead singer who could put such people as Brian McKnight and Beyoncé to shame. But even with all this talent and great management, a well-oiled management team, the best talent agent, and everything else that you could possibly need to become successful in the music industry, the bottom line is "are your original compositions good?" What I mean by that is no matter how great your band is in live performances and more, if the original songs you've written and are performing live aren't good, your success will most assuredly be cut short. A good song can stand the test of time as has been proven by some of the best songwriters such as a Paul McCartney, Stevie Wonder, Paul Simon, James Taylor, and many, many more. You see we are trying to make livings in an environment where television and other industries will dictate much of what we wear, what we drive, what we eat, who we date, who we don't date, the type of friends we associate with, and more. It may seem to you that television does not have this type of control over you, but ad agencies do not spend billions and billions of dollars each year because they do not know what they're doing! These individuals are gifted at knowing what the public wants and doesn't want, and if the public doesn't know what it wants ... they will dictate that for you. The same is true with radio play. Do you really think that the music we hear on the radio are the songs that we choose to listen to? Do you really think that the songs that we hear on digital radio are the songs we've chosen to listen to? Do you think that the songs on the Billboard charts with a bullet or that are in the top 20 or top 10, or songs that are on the Hot 100 are there because they are great tunes? I'm asking you this question because sometimes the answer is yes they are great tunes. But you know as well as I do that there've been songs on the radio that we all wonder how in the world could that thing have ever made it to airplay? Or, how could that artist be where they are when I've seen so many bands just in my local area that would blow them out of the water? The answer, my friends, is ... Marketing! We'll get into this in another chapter.

BACK TO THE BASICS

Let's get back on track. The bottom line is good songs stand the test of time; good songs will succeed on the radio in getting airplay and being put on medium to heavy rotation. A good song has the greatest chance of success. So when you or your band mates are together in your practice room, be it in the basement of your parents' home, dorm room on campus, or one of the practice rooms at a music store, try to write the very best songs you can. Those songs will have a key ingredient known as familiarity. If you can tap into the listener's memory and bring forth an emotion that they felt in the past or are currently feeling, you have a very great chance of having a successful recording. So many songwriters whom I have met in the industry, books that I've read on songwriting, and the many performers you meet on the road will all tell you the same thing: "It's got to be a great song, if you plan on making it in the industry." This is why I stated that the more you write, the better your chances are that maybe one out of 50 or 100 tunes—let me be a little bit more magnanimous and say 10 out of 100 songs—that you have written could be a hit. Don't stop writing. I'll close by saying this: If you think it's hard now to get gigs, to make a living out of performing music, wait until you get signed! You'll need to work 10 times harder than you ever worked before so you can stay in the coveted position that every other musician on the planet wants, and would be willing to do almost anything to get it from you.

CHAPTER 2

Managers, Agents and Attorneys

The successful artist typically puts together a professional team consisting of the following:

- Personal Manager—the all-important personal manager stays on top of everything the artist does
- Business Manager—handles financial transactions for the artist
- Road Manager—deals with the specifics of concerts and touring
- Agent—finds gigs for the artist
- Attorney—negotiates contracts, provides expertise in areas of contract law and copyright
- Publisher—works with the artist's songs and tries to get them placed into other artists' recordings and with other outlets such as films and television music
- Publicist—works on public relations (PR) and advertising campaigns for the artist

MANAGERS

Right about the time that an artist begins to consistently make enough money from local and regional shows to support themselves, and when they get serious about a getting a record deal, is the time for a personal manager. A delicate dance exists because the manager wants to get involved with an already established act that can generate income immediately. Hopefully a manager sees enough potential in a new artist to take them on. Managers work on commission of 10%–20% for a one- to three-year time period, depending on the manager's track record. The more successful the artist, the more commission the manager earns. The manager's primary function is to advance the artist's career. The manager's income is generated from recordings, live concerts, publishing, and any other income source related to music and entertainment. In order to make this happen, the manager must first hire a lawyer, then create the rest of the team of individuals required to get the artist's career going, and then maintain career momentum.

The manager is the key member and general manager of an artist's team of personnel and must have a relationship with the artist based on strong personal ties and trust. The artist needs to know that the manager is doing everything he/she can do to further the artist's career, and the manager needs to know that there is going to be enough money coming in to get a decent commission from the artist's great work. The manager creates a business plan, strategic plans, and goals, all to win public recognition and of course, turn a profit—the manager does not work for charity. When the band or artist makes money, the manager makes money. Keep in mind that the manager's 10%–20% of gross income must make enough to cover the manager's expenses (such as office staff and all supplies) and have enough left to put money into the manager's pocket. This is why managers will want to manage as many acts as they can possibly handle—the more successful artists on the manager's roster, the more money comes in.

The manager should be completely familiar with all aspects of the music industry simply because as the key individual of the team, the manager will have to deal with every facet of the music industry for their artist. Managers should also be very familiar with the artist's market, as well as distribution and promotional systems in place for such an artist. Managing a pop diva will have major differences in marketing strategy as opposed to a death metal act. The manager is responsible for all of the artist's financial transactions and keeps a close eye on expenses since the manager will be taking in income and writing checks for the artist. Once there is enough income to warrant it, the manager also contracts for financial personnel such as a knowledgeable CPA to take care of taxes (and the various deductions musicians can take). Bookkeepers, financial planners, and business managers are also brought in to help with the artist's investments and to make sure the artist is financially sound, especially at the end of their career and in slow periods during their career.

The artist–personal manager relationship is based on belief in the artist's star potential and talent level. The manager will want from the artist a complete commitment of a long-term career since it won't do a manager much good if the artist or band hangs it up after a year. Other attributes of a personal manager are things such as being well organized, being an effective communicator and good writer, and having good music industry contacts. Also, the personal manager should have the creative ability to contribute to things like choosing the right songs for the artist and choosing the other members of the artist's team. The artist–manager relationship should be personal in nature as well—the manager will at times counsel the artist and at times simply be a friend for bouncing ideas off.

Once the artist–manager contract is negotiated, the manager must begin to market the act by using industry contacts to bring on voice/talent coaches, choreographers, image consultants, and others in order to create a professionally polished act ready for public consumption. The manager might also at this point start to look for material—songs for their artist to perform, even if the artist writes most of their own material (you can never have too many really good songs!). Additionally the manager must also find and contract for other key personnel such as a band to back the artist, sound crew to make the artist sound great in concert, and producers who work in the studio to make the artist sound great on recordings. Other people the manager must handle are PR and advertising firms dedicated to putting out a consistent message about the artist, as well as "branding" the artist. Furthermore, the manager also contracts for people such as graphic designers to create logos and CD artwork, printers to make promotional materials, mastering studios to put the final polish on recordings and videos, etc. Good managers should have everyone involved in the artist's career at their fingertips.

The manager's most important task is first to get an attorney who will represent the artist in all contractual negotiations, and then get their artist signed to a record label. Furthermore, record labels usually don't deal with artists directly. They would rather see a professional handling the affairs of any artist they are interested in signing. This is probably the most difficult task facing the manager ... established managers can get it done without too much trouble, upstart managers have a difficult time breaking through. Managers should come up with a strategic marketing plan for choosing a record label and for finding a way to get the best and most appropriate label for their artist. Managers must use every contact and advantage they can, and are hopeful to draw upon on a successful track record of getting other artists signed to a record deal. The label executive is also going to look for star potential in the artist, as well as the label's own financial stability, and even determining if they have a "need" for an artist in the particular music genre. In any case, it falls upon the manager to convince the power brokers of record labels to get in financial bed with his/her artist. Many artists engage a manager primarily for this purpose.

Once a record deal is landed, the manager becomes even more important in terms of first furthering, and then maintaining the momentum of the artist's career. Such activities include negotiating for higher and higher fees for performances, as well as looking out for ways to produce peripheral income. Additionally, the personal manager hounds the record company to coordinate PR and advertising campaigns, and hounds them in general to make sure the label is doing its job to take care of the artist's promotional needs. The manager should also be all over the PR firm to constantly get the message out there about the artist, and the publisher—the important player in creating income from the artist's songs, which in many cases is the largest source of income. Another important task for the manager is to make sure all promotion is coordinated because so many different entities are involved. The record label might be solely interested in getting airplay, while the agent might be solely interested in making money at live events—the two should be coordinated so that airplay, live events, record sales, marketing, and PR all come together simultaneously for every event in which the artist participates.

After the record deal, the manager finds the best agent to represent the artist. Research is required—the manager should speak to other artists about the talent agency in question. Other ways to research are to talk to venue owners about how well the agency delivered artists, and perhaps talk to other managers who may have worked with the particular agency. The agency should be able to deliver the most substantial work that furthers the artist's profile, as well as maximizes fees, and accurately represent the artist's drawing power within regions and segments of the population. Live-performance drawing power is really the key to this equation, for it is drawing power that sells tickets, and therefore makes money.

The manager advances the career of an artist by establishing and maintaining good relationships with key personnel and power brokers in the music industry, such as attorneys, producers, and promoters. Keep in mind that most of the music industry power brokers know each other on a first-name basis. When the manager needs to call on one of these people for help, hopefully the power brokers (or at least their assistants) will take the call. The manager must also make decisions regarding performances, how many, what kind, estimated size of the audience, etc., and make sure that performances are appropriate to the individual artist's direction and style, as well as for the target audience.

The manager must also develop a network of contacts and friends within the mass broadcast media outlets—music video and concert channels (such as MTV and VH-1 ... do they even play videos any more?), television networks, radio stations, music press (writers and publications that focus on music and entertainment fields). These entities are given promotional packs (promo packs) that highlight the artist—bio, press clippings, picture (important!), song samples, even video—and then are encouraged to write about or feature the new artist. Hopefully, the record label will use its publicists to promote the sale of recordings as the artist travels around the country by holding press events (a.k.a. parties with free food and drinks). The manager can then set up interviews for the artist. It may also be necessary for the manager to hire an independent PR company to promote their artist (for a price, of course).

FINANCES AND ARTIST–MANAGER AGREEMENTS

First of all, the management–artist contract should be negotiated by an attorney hired by the artist, and not working with the manager, as this would create a conflict of interest. The contract for a manager is usually vague, using clauses like "the manager will put forth his best effort to advise and counsel the artist in order to further the career of the artist." This kind of clause is difficult to quantify into real numbers. The agreement, therefore, might contain benchmarks that encourage the manager to hustle, such as higher commissions when more and more money comes in. For example: Up to the first $250,000 of income, the manager makes 20%, and once that artist's income shoots above $250,000, the manager makes 25%. Generally, the agreement is that the personal manager handles all of the artist's money ... what comes in and what goes out, taking commission on any money coming in. Additionally, the management contract can give the manager power of attorney—the ability to engage in contracts without the signature of the artist. This puts great responsibility into the hands of the manager, and sets the manager up for a lawsuit if he handles money poorly or for his own interests over and above the management percentage. (An example of being shady would be if the manager invested the artist's money in the manager's own personal financial interests.) For situations involving lots of money coming in, both parties may agree to hire the services of a business manager to take care of receipts and disbursements. Commission usually stems from all income (gross) the artist earns including anything of value such as royalties, income from publishers, or stock in a company. It is to the artist's advantage to define a commission base, which means limiting commissionable income to the artist's actual income and not items that might stem from money coming in for making videos or tour support since both of these items are recoupable by the label. More on this can be found in the record deals chapter.

Accountants are usually chosen during the formative stages of an artist–manager relationship. An accounting firm specializing in entertainment accounting and perhaps even international finance would be the first choice. The manager and artist would then agree on how they will stay in control of the accounting and tax reporting. Major artists will need an independent auditor to make sure the accountants and the personal manager are all completely above board and doing their job in a professional manner. Usually contracts will stipulate the conditions for an audit (as in how often) as well as who has to pay for the independent audit (usually the artist).

The going rate for the manager is 10%–20% of all money coming in the door, before taxes and expenses. Big-time managers can command 25% to as much as 50% (ouch). The idea is that since the manager has become responsible for forwarding the artist's career, the manager should be able to collect a percentage of the income. The percentage is typically set according to:

1. The stature of the manager—managers with good track records get higher percentages.
2. How much artist income exists—sometimes the more the artist makes, the lower the management percentage. In this case, a lower percentage of a lot more money is more advantageous than a larger percentage of less money.
3. How much service the manager is providing—are all services such as business management, accounting, and promotion done by the manager or by other entities?

It is very important to keep an eye on income and expenses ... 20% for the manager, 10% to the agent, and 10% to a lawyer on contingency add up quickly to up to 40% off the top of all money coming in! The personal manager should advise their client to be very careful about expenditures ... ultimately, however, the artist should be well informed of money coming and going, and should have the opportunity to approve of any spending.

Some personal managers will loan their artist money to keep them afloat during the beginning of their career and then make sure they get all of that money back (plus interest of course) once money is available. Some managers will even fund the first recording the artist makes in order to get the artist "out there" to show sales and popularity before going to a record label. This could quickly get out of hand, where the artist is beholden to the manager for the loan and the commissions and never makes any money for themselves. Hopefully, when the manager secures a publishing deal and a record deal, any such loans can be paid back in full from advances to the artist.

Much like the large agencies, large artist management companies will typically have a sub-manager handling the everyday business of the artist, with a top manager who comes in when important decisions are to be made or important actions are to be done (such as landing the initial record deal). Sometimes the sub-manager will want to go out on his or her own, and might want to take the artist with them. A "key person" clause might be used so that if a manager leaves a management company and goes out on their own, then the artist can choose to go with them. Artists may also want to change management, especially when the artist feels like he/she can get better support, give up less of a commission, or have better industry contacts through the new manager. This becomes a problem because the income that stems from the previous manager's work continues to flow—and the old manager will still want to be paid on that income. Of course the new manager wants to be able to tap as much commissionable income as possible, which may be difficult to do if the old manager is still collecting from deals he negotiated. Management contracts exist that stipulate that all income negotiated by the old manager would go to the old manager in perpetuity (in other words, forever). The compromise is usually a gradual process of the old manager getting less and less and the new manager getting more and more of the commissionable income, otherwise known as a de-escalation. An amicable parting of artist and old manager to a new manager may be negotiated over a period of time. Perhaps the overlap would be extended for two years ... in the first 6 months the old manager would keep 75% of income and the new manager would get 25% of income from commissions ... then for the next 12 months each would get 50% of the total income from commissions, and for the last 6 months the old manager would get 25% and the new manager would get 75% of all income from commissions.

Many artist managers reside in California or New York and must abide by laws governing talent management in the particular state. In California, the law states that managers can only advise and counsel their clients, and cannot procure employment; otherwise they would have to be a licensed talent agent. In reality, personal managers work so closely with the artist that some procurement of employment occurs and this law is not closely observed or enforced. New York law defines "agents" as those who procure employment other than incidental to the manager. This way of defining agents allows the manager to procure incidental work for the artist; therefore, the New York law is more relaxed than the California law.

AGENTS

The primary function of the agent is to find work for their performers by offering talent to concert promoters, club owners, college concert presenters, convention planners, and anyone seeking music talent to perform at their show or event. Generally, agents will have a roster of clients they work with. They will also have a contact list of people who buy the talent. Essentially, the talent buyer describes or decides on the type of music they want and agents come up with an act from their roster of artists. The agency then decides on how much money it will charge the buyer, then the agent gets a commission in return for getting the work for the artist. The agency is then responsible for collecting from the promoter, and for paying the artist the net from the gross fee (the gross fee minus commission and expenses). The tricky part of an agent's job is to find a balance between how much money the artist should get and how much the buyer can pay out, and to make enough profit from the commission. According to Diane Rapaport, "Talent agents are under pressure to ensure profits from three businesses: themselves, their clients and the buyers of talent." Diane Rapaport, *A Music Business Primer* (New Jersey, Prentice Hall, 2003). 147. Agents make money by working on commission, taking a portion of what the artist makes on the gig that the agents get for the artist. Typically the commission rate for agents is 10%–20% of the gross income. Agents are also able to deduct reasonable expenses from gross income.

There are different agencies that work on local, regional, and national levels. Some agencies are really just one person working to connect talent and talent buyers. The big players in the game of finding work for artists are giant international companies with hundreds of big name artists on their roster. Such companies are William Morris, International Creative Management (ICM), and Creative Artist's Agency (CAA). These big boys (and most other agencies) require their artists to be completely exclusive, meaning that the artist gets gigs from only that particular agency and no others. It also means that the agency collects a commission on all work performed by the artist whether the agency booked it or not. The good news is that talent agencies do not collect commission on money coming in from recordings or publishing. Exclusivity to a local or regional talent agent could become a problem if the act is ready to go nationwide—the local or regional agent may not have national contacts to book the group. Usually the artist will try to specify in the contract that the agency can collect only on work involving music performances and appearances, and not for things like acting roles in a movie or television show. If the performer were to contract with an agency for acting for example, and did not have the aforementioned "out" clause, then the artist would have to pay two agencies—this is called a double hit or a double commission, and of course is not to the artist's advantage.

Start-up agents work with local clubs and bars, and with local artists, trying to make a name for themselves in a particular region. As their artists draw more and more people to the clubs and bars, the agency can ask for more money for their artist, which in turn generates more money for the agent's commission. In direct contrast, start-up local and regional artists sometimes will book themselves, dealing with all of the hassle of self-booking—the repeat phone calls, contracts, pricing, double and triple checking with the club or venue about specifics, etc., but without giving up the 10%–20% commission. When income level permits, artists tend to be much better off going with a talent agent and avoiding the hassles of booking themselves. There are also non-exclusive agents who possibly work without an artist–agent contract. Such an agent would simply procure work for the artist and take commission on whatever work they get for the artist, without exclusivity. Such types of agents might also work on only a specific concert or tour that might feature a number of different artists (such as a large festival like Bonnaroo or a tour like Ozzfest).

When searching for an agent, or considering an agent's offer, it is important that the agent knows what kind of work the artist can deliver, and the artist must be confident in the track record of the agent. In the process, the artist can contact other artists represented by that particular agent and call clubs booked by the agent in order to get an idea of the agent's effectiveness and professionalism.

According to Dick Weissman, the tasks performed by an agent include:

- Making dozens of calls and follow-up calls.
- Making sure contracts are received, well in advance of the actual date.
- Collecting substantial deposits on jobs, especially if the agent has never previously done business with a promoter or club manager.
- Making sure the act's publicity is well written, attractive, and current.
- Dealing with the college market, where a student may control what artists perform, and the person holding that position changes from year to year.
- Buying tickets for the band, making sure that transportation is as cheap as possible, and providing the artist with clear and specific information about where they are going.
- Double-checking all aspects of the contract, such as the name of the building, the time and date of the performance, the length of the show, the sound system, and so on.
- Making sure there is a provision for accommodation in the contract that specifies whether the act gets single rooms or that a particular hotel or motel chain be used.
- Carefully examining the contract for any restrictions on the geographic area where the band can appear on the same tour.
- In the case of clubs, is there a provision that allows the owner to book the act again? If so, is there something in writing that provides for increased income for future bookings?
- Does the contract specify a time for equipment load-in, and a time for a sound check, well in advance of the show?
- Is there a provision for selling band merchandise? Will the band have to find someone to staff the merchandise table, or will the promoter provide someone? Does the contract state that the promoter or hall receives a percentage of any merchandise sales?
- Is there clear and specific information about payment? For example, 50% on signing the contract, 50% in cash or certified check on completion of the engagement. If there is a percentage on top of the guaranteed payment, does it clearly define what constitutes legitimate deductible promoter expenses, such as advertising, the number of free tickets to the press, and hall rental?

Dick Weissman, *Understanding the Music Business.* (New Jersey, Prentice Hall, 2010) 58–59.

All contracts with legitimate agencies stipulate that the artist must approve of any gig that the agency delivers and have a termination clause, which allows the artist to leave the agency if they can't find work for the artist for a set period of time (usually 3–4 months).

For tours, the agency must be wary of routing, meaning stringing dates along in a logical geographic sequence rather than scattered all over the country on consecutive days. Proper tour routing is essential for the touring group, as show after show can wear an artist down, especially if there is excessive travel between shows.

Agents usually have a special relationship with colleges and universities. Such venues are generally more suited for music listening (as opposed to a club, which can be more of a social setting). Colleges typically have a student program board that is in charge of booking acts to perform on the campus. In many cases, the program board is made up of students, with different students each year booking the shows. Colleges are great for breaking new artists, in that they are usually hungry for new music in addition to the artists with more drawing power. Also, college program boards are funded each year, and they don't necessarily have to turn a profit, as long as they break even. This kind of arrangement can mean more money available for the artist. The National Association for Campus Activities (NACA) holds regional and national conventions that showcase talent for the program board staff of all colleges who attend. Most artists pay a fee to showcase at these events or simply to have a convention booth available in order to promote themselves to student decision-makers. Some colleges in a particular region will try to negotiate a block booking, giving the artist a string of performance dates in a region, all for a reduced artist fee. In other words, they offer the artist good routing for a price break. The agents involved must use care in such bookings to make sure the artist is making enough money for the block booking to be feasible.

An interesting way artists can book themselves is through a company called Sonic Bids (www.sonicbids.com). The artist pays a yearly membership fee as well as application fees for various shows and festivals, hoping to be chosen by the concert promoter running the event. At the time of this writing, Sonic Bids is accepting submissions for the College Music Journal's concert series, the CMJ Music Marathon in New York City.

Another interesting system involves a booking agent who puts together bands in a particular region, usually for bar mitzvahs, weddings, conventions, or any social gathering that calls for live musical entertainment. The band leader or other central figure will have dozens of capable musicians at his disposal to put together bands at the various events. The musicians will get at least union-scale wages, and the bandleader takes whatever money is left over from the booking after paying the musicians. Many times the bands specialize—rock band, variety band, mariachi band, etc. For events like New Year's Eve, this could be a lucrative opportunity—multiple bands performing will mean multiple streams of income, and the high demand will allow the bandleader to charge more for each event.

As an artist progresses through their career, they might decide to go to a different agency because they might not feel like they are getting enough agency attention, and are getting lost among the agency's huge roster of artists. To combat this, agencies will typically assign one person from their company to deal with a single artist or a select few, and that way the artist feels like they are getting the agency's full attention. This person is called a "key person," and an artist can specify in the agency

contract that a key person be used. If one of the agency's agents decides to go it alone, the key-person clause would give the artist the opportunity to go with the agent. Since this kind of thing happens all the time, agencies might make their agents sign a contract with non-compete clause, saying that if the agent leaves, he or she will not work as an agent for a specific period of time, say two years.

One trick to look out for, according to Dick Weissman, is a double booking, where the agent books an artist for one price negotiated with the artist, and a much larger price negotiated with the talent buyer. In this situation the booking agent simply pockets the difference—sometimes up to 50% above the rate given to the artist. This kind of shady activity is, of course, frowned upon by the various unions franchised by the agent.

In California and New York, agents representing artists have to be licensed by the state in order to work. This is to prevent the cigar-smoking wise guy from taking too much commission or otherwise abusing their artists by having them do too many not-so-great gigs. Most legitimate agents are franchised by the various artist unions and guilds, which limits the agent's commission usually to 10%, and 15% for some special cases. Also, the unions require that the agent not be engaged in other artist-related activities (such as acting as a personal manager and getting a double commission: One as an agent and the other as a manager). The unions and guilds require term limits for agencies, usually 1–3 years, so the artist can decide to go with another agency if they choose. The unions involved are typically as follows:

AFM—(American Federation of Musicians) provides an exclusive agent–musician agreement
AFTRA—(American Federation of Television and Radio Artists) dictates a standard exclusivity contract
AGVA (American Guild of Variety Artists) has a required exclusive agency contract

ROAD MANAGER

Another member of the artist's team is the road manager. Primarily, the road manager ensures that all things directly related to putting on the show and the tour operate smoothly and efficiently. The road manager stays in constant contact with the talent agent booking the shows so that everything for the next show is handled properly. This is otherwise known as "advancing" for the next show on the tour. On the show at hand, the road manager is responsible for making sure that the venue lives up to their end of the performance contract, including payment (most important) as well the technical details of putting on the show. Details are usually spelled out in a technical rider—a contract that goes along with the main contract from the agent. The technical rider spells out items such as:

- The size and quality of required sound system.
- The size and quality of the required lighting setup.
- Number and issuing of backstage passes.
- What kinds of food and drink will be provided at the venue for the artists.
- Number of persons required to help with load-in and load-out.
- Whether the venue must provide personnel to work the merchandise table.
- Appropriate parking areas for the tour bus or other transportation used.
- Amount of security personnel required backstage and in the venue.

The road manager takes on the responsibility of making sure hotel reservations and all travel arrangements for the artist and crew are made. Additionally, the road manager is responsible for hiring tour personnel such as sound and lighting technicians and other support persons. Road managers handle the entire touring group's "per diem," which is an amount of money given to each artist and crew member to cover food and other expenses each day while out on the road. In many instances, and since everyone on the tour represents "another mouth to feed" and an expense, the road manager will perform double duty such as operating the front-of-house console during the performance or serving as stage manager during the performance. Road managers are usually paid a salary during the time they are out on the road. It is not uncommon for experienced road managers to receive a yearly salary from the artist so that they are always "on retainer" for any shows booked for the artist. This way the artist is ensured that the road manager will always be available and will not have to compete with other artists vying for the road manager's services. Road managers must stay in constant contact with whoever is underwriting the tour, and keep accurate financial records of all money coming in and going out while out on the road. Ultimately, the idea is to take as much responsibility as possible away from the artist and allow the artist to concentrate on putting on a great show.

BUSINESS MANAGERS

When enough revenue starts coming in regularly, a business manager is often brought in to the team. Business managers are usually CPAs (certified public accountants) who have graduated with an accounting/business degree and have passed the CPA exam. Business managers handle the finances for the artist, including income, outflow, profit and loss statements, and paying appropriate taxes. Business managers will also advise their clients on good investment opportunities in cases where substantial money is coming in. Also, once the money is coming regularly, it is a good idea to put band and crew on salary—the business manager will take care of all payments and subsequent employment taxes that must be paid. Business managers are able to run audits on the various royalty-producing entities, primarily the publisher and record label, to make sure all money due the artist is being paid. Accountants need accurate records of financial transactions, so they must rely on accurate record keepers such as the personal manager and the road manager when touring. In return for the business manager's services, the agreement is usually 5% of gross income when such income rises over an agreed-upon flat fee. The artist should be able to check up on the business manager and run an independent audit to make sure all of the business manager's activities are in the best interest of the artist.

ATTORNEYS

Entertainment attorneys are not a necessary evil, in fact they are some of the most powerful and helpful people in the music industry. Most entertainment attorneys are very skilled at negotiating the various contracts involved with the music industry, and are very knowledgeable about copyright law and intellectual property.

Many entertainment attorneys are routinely connected to the various "movers and shakers" within the industry simply because they work with those people to negotiate contracts on the behalf of artists or for record labels, publishers, promoters, etc. With their industry connections, attorneys are able to perform some of the tasks that personal managers might do, such as get an artist access to a recording label's A&R people. In fact, many A&R and other label executives have much respect for good entertainment attorneys and might trust their opinions more than someone coming off the street representing themselves. For example, an entertainment attorney might be able pass a demo recording to a label executive simply because he has direct access. Labels want to play nice with attorneys because attorneys regularly negotiate contracts either for labels or for artists negotiating with the label, all depending on the client.

In general, entertainment attorneys have an hourly fee they charge (usually hundreds of dollars per hour). Other payment options might be negotiated with an attorney such as contingent fees (if an attorney's artist gets signed, then the attorney collects from any kind of advance, which of course, the attorney negotiates for the largest amount possible). Other arrangements might be that an attorney will take a percentage of an artist's gross income such as 5%–10% if the attorney is the person responsible for getting an artist a "deal," therefore acting as a manager for the artist.

An attorney should not represent both sides in a contract negotiation. This kind of thing is called a "conflict of interest," where it is to the attorney's advantage to work both sides of the fence. Both sides of a negotiation should have their own attorney. Another conflict of interest might arise for attorneys who also function as publishers or managers, since the attorney would be getting a commission as a manager, and also a commission as the attorney in a contingency deal! Such agreements are frowned upon by bar associations.

Discharging an attorney must be done in writing of course. However, an attorney who has a contingency deal with an artist would still want their commission even though they are no longer the client's attorney. This kind of situation must be resolved, usually with yet another attorney! Most would agree, in this case, to a graduated de-escalation of fees similar to what a departing personal manager might get.

In cases of copyright violation (where someone copied too much of someone else's song) entertainment attorneys will prosecute for or defend their client. There have been a number of examples where copyright infringement has been litigated in courts. At the time of this writing, a most recent example involved the group Coldplay and guitarist Joe Satriani. Satriani felt that the Coldplay song "Viva La Vida" was a close rip-off of his song "If I Could Fly." Attorneys from both sides decided to settle out of court.

Attorneys also act as arbitrators and mediators. In this capacity, it is the attorney's job to try to get two sides to agree on terms to settle their disputes amicably and out of court. Arbitration is generally a binding agreement, meaning the parties must live by the arbitrator's decisions. Mediation is a less formal process and merely suggests solutions to disputes. Many contracts include an "arbitration clause" that stipulates disputes first go to arbitration before going to the court system. Obviously the attorney performing the arbitration or mediation should not also represent any side of the dispute.

Finding an entertainment attorney is relatively easy if you are in one of the recording centers of the U.S. It is a good idea to check an attorney out before getting into a relationship. You can talk to other clients, see if he has experience in the type of negotiation or service you are looking for, and check to see if in general he seems knowledgeable on copyright law and intellectual property. Another way to check attorneys out is through the American Bar Association, which should have at least some information on the attorney in question.

CHAPTER 3

Record Company Contracts

Record companies have been in existence in the United States since the early 1900s. A record company's primary purpose is to sell records recorded by the musical acts that are signed to that particular record company. Obviously, it is far more complex than that. What I would like to do in this chapter is to define some of the specifics that are contained within a record contract that I hope every professional will be aware of. But, I know that there are many who are entering the music industry, and especially those who are in various music-industry classes, who are unaware of the specifics of record contracts. So let's begin.

Today, record companies in the United States generally fall into two major categories: The Majors and the Indies or Independent Record labels. Some in the music industry would say one of these record labels would have distinct advantages over the other. Let's quickly discuss these differences. The major labels in the United States are consolidated into four large conglomerates. These conglomerates are Universal Music Group, Sony/BMG, Warner Music Group, and EMI. EMI is in the process of restructuring due to the mishandling of its owner Guy Hands. There are several subsidiary labels that are associated with these major conglomerates such as Capitol, Blue Note, and Virgin records, which are, or I should say were, subsidiaries of EMI (we'll see what happens after the restructuring of EMI). Geffen, Interscope, PolyGram, and Motown are subsidiaries of Universal Music Group. RCA, Columbia, Arista, and others are subsidiaries of Sony/BMG. Finally, Atlantic, Elektra, and Warner Bros. Records are subsidiaries of the Warner Music Group. These companies within the conglomerates account for over 87% of retail sales in the United States. One important item we should note is that the United States is the largest producer and consumer of entertainment products and entertainment is America's largest export (Diane Rapaport). Once a business entity declares itself a "record company," several business parameters must be fulfilled. This business entity is now responsible for the making of the recording, the manufacturing of a recording, the distribution of the recording, the sales and marketing of the recording, and more. One reason I bring this detail to the forefront is that there are many educational institutions that will start a project and then call themselves a record company. This is something I would recommend not doing, unless you are familiar with entertainment law, because of the requirements you are obligated to fulfill.

One major advantage to signing to a major label is that of distribution. Even though the recording industry is quite erratic these days, it is well known that the majors have established many influential contacts over several decades. The old saying "it's not what you know, but who you know" still applies. However, I think that this saying needs to be amended to "it's not what you know, or who you know ... But who wants to know you!" Though the industry is very large, it is a close-knit community and news, be it bad or good, travels quickly within its members. Therefore, you may know some influential people, but if they don't want to know you or work with you, it means nothing.

INDIE LABELS

Independent labels started to develop when the major record companies were not seeking specific genres of music. Musical stylings such as Bluegrass, Jazz, Gospel, New Age, Christian, and other music indigenous to certain parts of the country seem to be ignored by the major record conglomerates. Intuitive businessmen picked up on this fact and began their own independent record labels to give musicians an opportunity to record and sell their product through independent distributors that drew the attention of niche markets. In the beginning, the major record companies had many more connections within the industry than the independent labels had, so independent record labels collaborated within distribution areas. According to the 2010 Grammy awards statistics, independent label artists outsold major label artists for the first time in recording history. Musical artists such as Anni DiFranco, The Gaithers, and many other musical acts soon begin their own labels because their music, their draw, or their followings have not developed enough for larger labels to sign them. However, this should not discourage any reviewer reading this because, depending on distribution and marketing strategies, many independent artists who market themselves can make almost as much money as major artists signed to larger label deals. In the beginning, distribution deals worked out between the Independent and Major labels, but now that Independent labels are beginning to usurp the market share of the Majors, we see a shift in that dynamic. It used to be said that artists would go with an Independent label because they would receive more personal attention, a greater affinity for their art and music, and a stronger understanding of their audience base than they would have received from a Major label. I can speak from experience that this was not always the case. The bottom line is this, if you have written a good song, if you have written a good album, regardless of what label you're signed with, good music will stand the test of the market and of time. Early on Independent labels have a small, insignificant market share. As new genres of music developed in the United States, particularly on the East Coast in Queens and the West Coast in Los Angeles, Hip-Hop and Rap music developed in the streets of African-American neighborhoods. With the assistance of forward-thinking producers such as Russell Simmons and Rick Rubin, as well as Dr. Dre and others, Hip-Hop and Rap music went from being local street music, to become a worldwide phenomenon. These two genres of music began much like the other styles of music in the independent-label arena.

An Independent label is a record company that is independently funded and not necessarily connected with any of the major labels. We musicians or future entrepreneurs within the music industry could start a home-based Indie label and possibly turn it into a highly profitable business venture. It was said that in the beginning, indie labels often faced an uphill battle trying to get their music heard on the radio. This is absolutely correct because they did not have the financial wherewithal to compete with the majors in the arena of Pay For Play, or what we know as Payola. We don't want to turn a blind eye to the fact that payola still exists in the music industry today as more and more artists' music is being discovered through live performances, the Internet, word-of-mouth, and many other resources. Despite their struggle, the labels have endured—not only have they survived, but they've arrived in the last 3 to 5 years and are assigning more and more successfully selling artists, obtaining more radio play, and are beginning to outpace the majors in total record sales and digital music downloads. In March of 2010, the Website known as *The Top 13* came out with a list of the most successful and largest independent record labels. Those labels included Sub Pop, Dischord, Factory, Touch and Go, Matador, Megaforce, Warp, Merge, and others. Many of the Independent labels featured genres such as Alternative music, Hip-Hop, and Rap. Most of your major rock and pop artists are signed with major labels, but this is changing quickly. The longer the major labels are in a state of disarray, the greater the opportunity for the Indie record labels to succeed by virtue of signing major, established rock and pop artists as well as newly discovered artists. When comparing the Major labels with the Independent labels, music aficionado Steve Albini said, "the Majors have a reputation for giving artists unfavorable deals and rewarding the business team greater than the artist who created the music." I completely agree with this statement; major artists from all genres of music have also expressed similar opinions. For example, Herbie Hancock, the world-renowned jazz pianist and in-novator of various musical technologies, shared his opinion on the major label business model: "I'm not happy about the business model that the record companies have been running until now. They have proven repeatedly that they are far from Angels, far from having even a casual interest in giving artists and songwriters a fair share. They have been ripping off artists, writers, and the public for close to a century, to the point where I can honestly say I don't trust them at all" (Alderman xvii).

Independent labels have also used the Internet far more than the major labels have in recent years. I think the reason for this is that Major labels have greater funding for market-ing than an Independent label does, therefore the Independent label must construct new and creative ideas for marketing their artists, which undoubtedly would incorporate the use of the Internet. This is not to say that the majors do not incorporate the Internet in their marketing strategies. What I am suggesting here is that when funds are not as available to one group within the music industry, then that group must modify its mode of operation and incorporate as many marketing strategies as are available to them.

Now that we have identified the two major players in the music industry as far as the two types of record labels operating within the music industry, let's discuss the details contained within record contracts for both the majors and independent record labels.

Unfortunately, like in any other growing industry in this country when a great deal of money can be made, certain people will want to maintain control of that business entity. To control the dissemi-nation of the music from its artists and the royalties earned, the record labels established regulations that were geared to favor the business entity as opposed to the artist. Prior to March 2002, most, if not all, record labels would hold a band under contract for an indefinite period. What this translates into is that the three or four most successful acts of a record company were the main money earners for the entire record label. Even though a label may have as many as 30 to 50 bands signed with them within the different departments and genres, only a few made money and sold enough units to keep the record company afloat. The musical acts that did not produce as well were either dropped and used as a tax write-off or the record company would continue their contract for a short period to earn money from mechanical royalties and then release the band from their contractual obligation. Because of a clause in their recording contract, the company would control the recording artists who earned the majority of the money for the record company. This clause would specify not a length of time that the band would be under contractual obligation, but their obligation to produce a certain number of recordings for the company for their contract to be complete. The problem behind this type of record contract is that the record company would delay the process of the completion of the number of recordings required in order to keep the band for an indeterminate amount of time, which held the band/musicians in an unfavorable contractual position. In other words, the musical acts were prisoners of the record company, and making the record company the majority of their earnings.

The bands that were the biggest moneymakers for the record companies, and generally the biggest draw for concerts had had enough! Many artists and entertainment attorneys congregated in our nation's capital for a Senate hearing convened in 2002 examining the contractual relationships between record companies and artists. Labor code section 2855 was amended to reflect the following: "labor code section 2855 protects workers in California by limiting to seven years the length of time they can be bound to an employer by a professional services contract." This was a huge win for recording artists as now they were no longer bound by the number of records they had to record for a recording company, and couldn't be compelled to a term exceeding seven years.

Record contract basics include a variety of legal parameters. I have said many times to colleagues, students, and local musicians, "the musician who represents themselves has a damned fool for a client." I'm going to discuss this particular issue in detail later on in the chapter; for now let's talk about the first thing to consider when negotiating a record contract: The "length of the contract." Record contract lengths can vary dramatically. Contracts were, and in many cases may be, determined by a variety of parameters ranging from the marketability of the band to how many songs the band or songwriter(s) have in the can when negotiating their record deal. Another factor that could determine the length of the contract is that of the band's draw. This concept of the draw is very important to understand. Draw is the ability to attract fans to your live performances; draw is the byproduct of a great live stage show, wonderfully written original music, a strong Web presence, and more.

THE MAIN POINTS IN A RECORD CONTRACT

The book *Music, Money and Success* by Jeffrey and Todd Brabec is a great book discussing many of the parameters of the music industry. In their chapter "Music, Money and the Recording Artist," they discuss the important points that are inclusive in almost every record contract. We'll review some of these points and discuss the variables that existed then and exist now in the industry.

I. TERMS

The time limit in which a record contract will last is structured around different variables dependent upon genre of music, current success of the artist signed, current economic structure, and the type of contract that is negotiated between the artist's manager and the record company. For example, the genre of music plays a huge role in the length of the contract, particularly if the genre is Rock, Pop, or Hip-Hop, and Rap. After speaking with many entertainment attorneys, it's a foregone conclusion that for Rap music, the business paradigm is that of "the quick kill." This is not to say that there aren't Rap artists who enjoy long and illustrious careers, but for the most part, the majority of rap artists are one-hit wonders. It is commonly known in the industry that most Rap music artists are sought after for the one hit that will generate the record company good money, after which they will drop the artist from their roster. I know that this sounds extremely cruel and unusual but it occurs often in the industry. The term of the contract can be determined by a length of time or by the number of records that the artist must record in order for the contract to be deemed complete. Other ways the Term can be defined would be as a distribution deal/contract wherein the record company will pay for distribution only after the artist has paid for the recording process, the mixing and mastering process, and the duplication process. Most, if not all, record contract Term agreements will have a built-in expiration clause to protect the record company, which will state that after a designated period if the artist has not produced a recording sufficient for marketing, the record contract will be void. There are also other stipulations that can be written into a record contract that will be discussed shortly.

II. ADVANCES

Contained within most record contracts is the Advance clause, which stipulates a monetary payment of a negotiated amount, which the record company will distribute to the artist upon the signing of the record contract. Every particular within a record contract is negotiable and the Advance which the artist could receive is highly negotiable. A variety of items could predetermine the amount of money the artist receives as an Advance. For example, a new artist receiving their first record contract would not receive a large Advance because they have not proven themselves as a viable commodity within the music industry. Conversely, an artist who has been in the industry for a period of time and has had great success could demand an extremely large Advance, as was the case when Donald Passman negotiated Janet Jackson's Velvet Rope album deal in which approximately $80 to $85 million dollars was paid to Janet Jackson as her advance. To date, the largest Advance paid to a recording artist is that of $120 million paid to Madonna when negotiating her deal with Sony Records. The record Advance can be calculated using different formulas within a recording contract. A common option is the one known as the "minimum/maximum" formula. This computation specifies the record company will calculate the actual advance for an option album or albums based on a percentage of the earnings generated by the artist's recently released prior album, and this percentage usually ranges from 50% to 75%. This is just one of countless variations in calculating an Advance for a recording artist. The monies received in an Advance, particularly for a newly signed act, are generally used for recording costs, or for paying off previous debts incurred from the negotiations to get the artist/band signed. Unfortunately, after the artist manager takes his or her percentage, the band members generally split the remainder of the Advance among themselves and spend it on personal items ranging anywhere from an automobile to musical equipment. A piece of advice for those of you who are one of the few, lucky artists or bands offered a record contract with an Advance, be smart with your money and use it to pay for recording costs. This will prevent these costs from being recouped through the mechanical royalties you will hopefully earn when your record is released.

III. ROYALTIES

This clause contained within the record contract is one of the most important, as it determines the amount of money the artist will receive from the sale of their recorded product. Royalties are negotiated not in a dollar amount, but in a percentage based on the wholesale or retail price of the artist's recorded material. There are a number of factors that will determine what this percentage will be based upon, certain contractual provisions negotiated by the record company and the band's entertainment attorney. There are five types of royalty schemes that are negotiated in a record contract (these royalty schemes will be discussed in the copyrights section of the book). Royalties are paid within a contractually agreed-upon amount of time after the record companies collect the monies earned from their distributors, retail outlets, and other entities. The record company will pay the composers of the intellectual property (song or songs) and the artist's publishers; these payments are known as mechanical royalties. Mechanical royalties are predetermined by a company called the Harry Fox Agency. This company sets a Statutory Rate, which is a predetermined amount of money that the songwriter will earn each time their song is performed. Currently the statutory rate is 9.1 cents for up to a 5-minute song. Now I know this may not seem like a lot of money to you, but if your song is on medium or heavy rotation with hundreds or thousands of radio stations across the country and/or world, you can make several hundreds of thousands of dollars per month from a single song.

Another factor to consider when looking at royalties is that of escalating royalty rates. Moreover, escalating royalty rate is a royalty that is adjusted upward that benefits the artist, predetermined by the number of sales of CDs or digital downloads the artist has of their album and/or song. For example, a scenario involving the earning of a 10% royalty for selling up to 250,000 units (song(s) or digital download(s)), after 250,000 albums, the royalty would escalate to 11% for 250,000 to 500,000 units. For sales of 500,000 to 750,000 albums, it could escalate to 12%, and then from 750,000 units and above sold, the royalty rate could escalate to 13% and most likely hold there.

Now for some bad news. There are costs that are incurred by the record companies that sometimes, well let's just say all of the time, must be paid back. Who pays this back? Why, you do. The artist. Through your royalties. What are some of these costs that the record companies will absorb in the beginning, but recoup later on? One is promotional costs. Major and Independent labels budget a large amount of money annually from the gross income for promotion, and selectively allocate funds according to sales projections for each artist. Promotional costs include the design of the CD inserts, promotional and packaging materials, press kits, EPKs (electronic press kits), Website design, and radio promotion; probably the largest amount of money allocated for promotional costs is that of advertising and other ancillary costs, all of which needs to be recouped by the record company. Then there are distribution costs. Now depending on the distribution company with which you sign a contract or the company with which the record companies themselves are directly affiliated, record producers, concert promoters, talent agents, and a variety of other music industry professionals have reciprocal agreements already in place long before you even begin negotiating with the record company for a contractual agreement. It is generally the case that record companies have standing relationships with specific distribution companies. Now, distribution costs are commonly 55% to 65% of the suggested list retail price. Other costs that work their way into the reduction of royalties are administration costs for the record company. Now depending on their scale of operations, administration costs can range anywhere from 15% to 45% of the record company's annual gross income. So, as you can see it's not cheap to run a record company. This is why when record contracts are negotiated with recording artists, the first two pages of a 100-page contract tell the artist what they will get and the other 98 pages state how all money earned belongs to the record company.

IV. CONTROLLED COMPOSITION CLAUSE

The controlled composition clause is one of the most hotly negotiated items within the record contract negotiations: It states who is in control of the intellectual property or song(s). I strongly recommend that all artists, songwriters, musicians retain control of their intellectual property and should have their legal person or team negotiate this. However, 99.5% of the time the record company will do everything in its power, legally speaking, to gain control of the artist's intellectual property.

The Controlled Composition Clause addresses how much money a record company will pay its recording artist (in his capacity as a composer) for those of his songs that he records. Thus, every musician who records for, or licenses or sells his or her self-produced master to a record company should analyze the Controlled Composition Clause carefully. Recently, the Controlled Composition Clause has become vastly more onerous, especially as used by the major record companies and thus should be carefully reviewed. (The Controlled Composition Clause: Is It Out of Control?, David Moser. *Entertainment, Publishing and the Arts Handbook*, 1997–1998 Edition, West Group). However, even in its more benign form, this clause needs to be evaluated. Typically the Controlled Composition Clause, in its more benign form, provides for the recording artist to grant his record company a mechanical license for the recording artist's own compositions at a reduced mechanical royalty rate than what currently is in effect.

A hypothetical example of this latter type of "benign"(??) Controlled Composition Clause reads as follows "... Record Company is hereby granted a mechanical license for all Controlled Compositions, as defined below, embodied in the Masters at fifty (50%) percent of the minimum statutory mechanical copyright royalty rate in effect on the date of first release of Records containing such Controlled Compositions (the 'Controlled Rate'). The term "Controlled Composition" means a Composition embodied in any Master delivered hereunder which is written or composed by Owner, alone or in collaboration with others, or is owned or controlled, in whole or in part, directly or indirectly, by Owner, or by any person, corporation, partnership, firm, or other entity in which Owner has a direct or indirect interest . ..."

In this type of Controlled Composition Clause, the recording artist is affected in two ways. First and foremost, the recording artist would only receive one-half (fifty percent) of the statutory mechanical royalty rate in effect. While seventy-five percent (75%) of the statutory mechanical royalty rate is more typical in this type of clause, fifty percent is not unheard of. Nevertheless, try to obtain as high a percentage as possible.

Secondly, the recording artist is also harmed in a less obvious manner. Because the mechanical royalty rate is pegged to the statutory mechanical royalty rate in effect at the time of "first release of Records," the artist will be harmed if the Record is sold many years after the contract is signed because the statutory mechanical royalty rate typically would be higher at that time. The statutory mechanical royalty rate is adjusted upwards every few years. Thus, even if the recording artist cannot cause the record company to delete this type of "Controlled Composition Clause," the recording artist should, in any case, seek to have the mechanical royalty rate pegged to the rate in effect at the date of manufacture of Records rather than at the date of first release of Records.

The type of Controlled Composition Clause places a monetary restriction, a cap, on the amount of mechanical royalties it will pay to the recording artist. In addition, should the record company be forced to pay more than its prescribed limit, the clause allows the record company to deduct such excess from the artist royalties (as opposed to mechanical royalties) it pays the recording artist. As mentioned above, this type of Controlled Composition Clause is being used by the major record labels more frequently today. A hypothetical example of this type of capped Controlled Composition

Clause reads as follows "... Recording Artist hereby grants and will cause all applicable publishers to grant to Record Company mechanical licenses in the USA at the rates set forth herein ('Controlled Composition Rate') with respect to musical compositions written, owned or controlled in whole or in part by any member of Recording Artist or a producer or by a company affiliated with any member of Recording Artist or Producer ('Controlled Compositions') and embodied on records distributed hereunder. In respect of Full Price records, the Controlled Composition Rate for all musical compositions regardless of length shall be seventy-five percent (75%) of the minimum USA statutory rate for selections whose timing is five (5) minutes or less; and with such Controlled Composition Rate being determined at the time of first release of records embodying the composition concerned, subject to the following configurationally ceilings for all musical compositions, whether or not Controlled: Nine (9) times the Controlled Composition Rate on Compact Disc Albums. In the event the actual aggregate mechanical copyright royalty rate paid by Record Company exceeds the maximum configurational ceiling for any record hereunder, Record Company shall deduct from any monies payable to Recording Artist hereunder (whether in respect of Controlled Compositions or otherwise) an amount equal to such additional payments. ..."

V. EXCLUSIVITY

According to Webster's dictionary, the term "exclusivity" is defined as "the quality or state of being exclusive," and "exclusive rights or services." An exclusivity clause that is contained within any contract basically means it is a restrictive agreement involving a good, services, marketing or market, or an area/territory that binds a principal and an agent in an association under which neither can make any similar deals with any other business entity or of the like, including other competitors. For our purposes within the music industry, I'd like to speak about exclusivity clauses in direct relation to recording contract agreements. Let's examine the exclusivity agreement or clause within the context of a relationship. For example, you're dating someone for a period of time, things are going well, you have many common interests, goals, aspirations, and of course, you are physically drawn to each other. There is going to come a time when one person will bring up the topic of exclusivity. That person will say, "I would like it if we dated only each other." Now you know when this statement is made, there will be certain extra conditions that will be included within this agreement or common goal. I don't think I need to get into the specifics of what those certain parameters are, as I know you are all very intelligent and already know where I would go with this.

An example that is more applicable for our purposes could be that of an agreement between an artist/band and an artist manager. We'll approach this from the perspectives of the band and of the manager. If a personal/artist manager is fortunate enough to find a band that is extremely creative in writing original material, performs live exceedingly well, and are all-around nice people who have a strong work ethic and are good to get along with, then a personal manager should have the wherewithal to want to sign an exclusive agreement with this act. The agreement would state they cannot pursue another personal-management contract or work in tandem with another personal manager. Equally, a band that has been in the industry for 2 to 3 years and has had the opportunity to work with a less-than-gifted personal manager will recognize the talents and benefits of a true leader. They would be foolish not to want to have an exclusive agreement signed with the gifted manager, as this agreement will ensure the band/artist proper representation to concert promoters, record label executives, and other important individuals within the music industry. Now as in everything within the music industry, there can be, and generally are, caveats in many areas. When considering signing an exclusivity clause or an agreement, it is to the benefit of the artist manager to have this agreement in place for a lengthy period. The reason behind this is that it can take up to two years to shape the band into a viable and marketable commodity, and make the necessary and appropriate contacts within the industry. Conversely, it is to the artist's advantage to sign a contract with an artist manager that is a maximum of two years with one-year options to be included at the end of their initial agreement for up to a period of seven one-year options. The reason behind this contractual agreement is that there are times when the artist manager either loses faith or lacks the desire to promote and manage the band to the best of their ability. I've seen this happen many times, and when this occurs and the band does not have some type of an option agreement in which they can opt out, then they are stuck with a manager who does not have their best interests at heart.

Now, how do we you apply this to a record contract/record company? The exclusivity clause primarily protects the record company. The amount of monetary investment from the record company is quite large for a band that they deem will be successful. When a company invests multi-millions into a person or band, it is in their best interest to protect their investment. In today's digital environment wherein the technology is so affordable, record companies can record a CD for less than $150,000 that can compete on the national and international markets. However, the major investment that a record company puts into an artist/band is that of marketing, which runs into the millions of dollars. Therefore, an exclusivity clause with an artist/band that they know will be successful is something they would be remiss in not including in the contractual agreement.

The term or length of an exclusivity clause will vary depending on the record company, the band or artist signed, the genre of music that is popular and selling at that time, and other parameters. This is a negotiable item within the exclusivity clause; however, rest assured that most if not all record contract agreements have an exclusivity clause. Exclusivity clauses will specify the songs that are written for that record company, rights to the use of the artist's/band's material for television or motion pictures, rights delineating ownership of copyright for the original material, and more. As a side note, make certain that you get everything in writing, have it reviewed by a qualified entertainment attorney, and make certain that both parties are in agreement with the materials contained in the contractual agreement. I've seen situations in which a personal manager is a friend or relative of one of the band members and no more than a handshake or a verbal agreement is given and accepted by both parties. Now legally, a verbal agreement is binding. However, should a conflict of interest arise, it's much easier to prove who was in the right when everything has been delineated in writing and signed by both parties and an entertainment attorney.

VI. CREATIVE CONTROL

Creative control is another extremely important contractual item that the artist or their personal manager should do their best to negotiate in their favor. Creative control is defined as a person, persons, or business entity that has control over the use of the intellectual property that the personal manager or entertainment attorney of the artist/band has given to the record company. This can include the variety of ways the song or songs may be used for the advancement and advertising of the band or artist to generate sales of their product. Creative control of an artist's intellectual property can stipulate that the publisher working with the record company has the right to change the actual melody or harmonic structure of the song as they deem appropriate for marketability. There are moral clauses that exist within publishing contracts that can specify the amount of change in which a publisher or record company can make to the artist's original creation, so you'll want to make sure that your personal manager or entertainment attorney will seek out the specific conditions that will be applied in the artist's favor. Creative control can be a very positive, revenue-generating portion of a recording contract. Yet, at the same time, how much creative control do the artists actually have after they've signed it over to a record company or an entity such as iTunes, Spotify, MySpace, and other online entities? On the site "DerekRoddy.com" the question was asked if an artist or band can truly maintain total creative control over their intellectual property, whether it's a song, recording, or another form. In other words, can you dictate to the record company what songs will go on the album, what songs will not go on the album, what the lyrical content of each song will be, which musicians will perform on the album, and much more? I really appreciate the answer that was given ... the answer was yes, if you release it independently. I suggest you read that sentence again. "If you release it independently." This means recording costs such as mixing, mastering, mass production, distribution, and the ever-so-expensive marketing are now on your shoulders! Are you sure you're up to the task? Many bands in today's music business environment are releasing independently. The key is finding a reputable and versatile distribution company, as well as working in tandem with a marketing agency. I think if you don't do these two things, it's highly unlikely that you'll have success. So now you have a decision to make. Do you let your personal manager shop for that major deal in which you can expect the record company to want creative control over your music? Or, do you do it yourself and take the risk of ongoing success or winding up in your 50s and 60s still playing the bars and small clubs in the town where you live? Tough choice ... I know.

VII. MASTERS

This is going to be a short one, ladies and gentlemen. At the risk of coming off too glib, if you have a contract signed with either a Major or Independent record label, it's a foregone conclusion that 99.998% of the time, the record company will own the master recording of the band/artist. I could end this section right here, but I'd like to give you some examples to explain why this is so.

Entertainment attorney Alan Korn in Berkeley, California, has a small online article with some fictional scenarios that help explain the issues relating to master recordings. First, understand that a master recording is generally a copyrighted work of a multi-track recording in which the band/artist has gone into the recording studio and recorded their original music. The medium they use, which is generally a hard drive, and this original music are then mixed and mastered; it is from this that CDs and other forms of music that are disseminated to the public are derived. The term Master can mean everything from a single song to an entire album or CD of songs that have undergone the process mentioned previously. I like to reference Alan Korn's scenarios concerning the ownership of the Master.

First, who owns the Master if the band breaks? I have discussed this scenario in almost every class I teach, as well as during private advising sessions. Generally speaking, it's not if the band is going to break up, but when. Therefore, if you go under this assumption, it is strongly advisable that you come up with an agreement prior to the band's being signed to any type of recording contract while you are still friends, so if this issue should arise the answer is already in writing somewhere. Alan Korn states "ownership of the band's sound recordings will likely depend on who is the author of these recordings." I would not make the mistake of stating that if you performed on the recording, then you are typically part owner of that recording. Generally, and contractually, the author of the song will be the owner of the sound recording. This is not always the case, as the record company generally owns the sound recording. However if you are not signed yet and your band has gone into the recording studio to record a demo, an EP, or a full CD, then the legal parameters change. In this situation, it's almost the unspoken agreement that the band in total has joint ownership in the recording. Again, my advice is not to assume this but to have something in writing; otherwise, the band members may have a strong case for part ownership.

A second situation is that of a band recording with a producer. I have never been in the recording studio where the producer did not have some input as to what should be played, overdubbed, mixed, or sampled for the song being recorded. If this occurs, does the producer then have co-authorship? Again, have something in writing! If you are working with a major label, it is highly unlikely that the producer of the album will claim any ownership of recording unless an agreement has been made with the band/artist. If the producer was asked to participate in contributing to the original song, the producer then has legal rights to that material. When this occurs, a rate or percentage is agreed upon to pay the producer as a work for hire or a percentage of royalties earned. However, record companies will generally, if not always, ask the record producer to sign a release form stating that they have no interest in relation to copyright to the master recording. To claim a copyright interest in any recording, the contribution made must include an appreciable amount of original authorship (Korn).

There have been situations in which a band will go into a recording studio owned by a friend or a colleague and negotiate free studio time with the understanding that they will reimburse the recording studio if the band becomes successful later on in life. Here we go again … the band and the recording studio have a falling out. Now who owns the rights to the Masters that happened to be in the studio's possession?

The above scenario could be construed as an oral contract, and as I stated previously oral contracts can be found binding in a court of law. However, in this situation Alan Korn states that the dispute involves whether or not the studio time was actually free. I've seen it in situations where the recording studio will maintain the control of the Masters if they feel they will not be compensated for their time and expertise given to record the band's music. However in the case of *Sound Dr. Recording Studio, Incorporated v. Conn*, 391 SO.2d 520 (La. 1980) (Korn), while both parties believed the studio would be compensated if the master tapes were released, the court found no actual agreement to release the tapes, and no expectations that the parties would continue their relationship until the tapes were released. Because the court found there was no agreement, it threw out the recording studio's lawsuit for compensation.

Another situation could be that of a Demo Deal, or a Distribution Deal. In situations such as these, the lines of ownership are not as blurred. Whether a moderate amount or even a minimal amount of monetary compensation is given to the band/artist, money has changed hands. Moreover, in a situation when money has changed hands, most of the time the company paying the artist will maintain ownership of the Masters.

The lesson you need to glean from this is to put something in writing before the band's success begins growing. The reason I state this is that when money becomes a factor in the band members' careers, personalities and people will change. Musicians, friends, high school buddies, everyone will put you in situations where very difficult decisions have to be made. When money is involved, traits that you were completely unaware of in individuals will begin to manifest themselves. To make a very long story short, put everything in writing before mounting success changes people.

VIII. ALBUM RELEASES (Live, Greatest Hits, Movie Sound Score)

Another item that is inclusive within a record contract is that of the release date of the recorded material. You do not want to be a Guns N' Roses-type band where you release a platinum-selling album, then take years to release your next album. Nothing short of the record company's filing bankruptcy will drive a record company out of its mind more than that situation. Therefore, record company contracts with bands/artists will have release dates that must be met or penalties will be assessed in the form of monetary compensation, reduced royalties, or worse: being dropped from the label. As a band or an artist, you need to remember that you have had your entire lifetime to draw experiences from for material for your first album. If this album is a success, and we hope it is, then the expectation of the record company is for you not to simply match the success of the first album but to outsell the first album. The scary thing is you only have about a year to accomplish that goal! Where do you plan to draw the material from for this album release? This is where being involved with a band that does collaborative writing will be helpful. Unless you have an extremely prolific songwriter and a band that can pump out songs right and left, eventually the creativity will dry up and so will your record contract.

Release dates can be determined by a variety of factors. For example, one of the best times to release any Hip-Hop, R&B, or Rap albums is in the months of January and February. February is Black history month and a very good time to release new albums by African-American artists. Other times that are advantageous to release albums are in the months of April and May, which precedes many of the outdoor concert events that occur during the summer months and when most students are out of school and able to attend these events. In addition, of course, the holiday season beginning around the end of October is a prime time for major artists to release their new albums. This is not necessarily the best time for a brand-new band or an Indie artist to release their new CD as you do not want to be competing against some of the biggest stars in the music industry.

Movie sound scores are generally released after the movie has been in the theaters for a period of 5 to 6 weeks. This is because if the movie is not successful, releasing a sound score would be a poor judgment call on the record label's part. Greatest hits albums are often preceded by a huge marketing and media blitz. The bands/artists that released these albums have a catalog of platinum-selling CDs or have a large cult following such as Frank Zappa, Tower of Power, and specific Jazz artists.

Put everything we've just discussed in the back of your mind—just lock it there for a while, and possibly dismiss it altogether. Here's why. The record industry is in a state of flux in which even the most seasoned professionals are trying to figure out what the next step is in relation to the dissemination of recorded music. So many established acts that the record companies would like to sign don't want to sign with a major or independent label. If the artist or band has a background in business and understands that the music industry is extremely erratic, then it is probably more advantageous for them to pursue a career on their own. The major record labels/conglomerates are laying people off in record numbers in Los Angeles, New York, and Nashville. Why would anyone at this time want to entrust his or her future with the label that might not exist a year from now? Yes, this is conjecture on my part, but many professionals in the industry whom I know in Los Angeles, New York, and Nashville have substantiated it.

The record industry is at such a point in its development, and they are losing money from circumstances involving digital audio downloads, that the record labels are involved in redesigning the standard record contract. Current talk in the industry involves what's known as the implementation of the 360-deal. The 360-deal is the record company's attempt to negotiate with its artists that it will not take as much in mechanical royalties as in the past. Instead, the record company wants to negotiate monetary compensation in the form of receiving a piece of the earnings from every aspect of the artist's/band's career, involving everything from concert ticket sales, merchandising, record sales, ancillary products such as clothing products, colognes and/or perfumes endorsed by the artists/bands, and more.

The response in the record industry by the artists is "No Way ... Not Now, Not Ever." Major record labels and conglomerates are downsizing to the point that music industry professionals in Los Angeles have communicated with me that the new trend will be known as Record Boutiques. Record Boutiques will be a business structure in which a minimum number of artists will be signed and managed by the record company. Moreover, the projections that I have seen and heard about have determined that the profits will be greater in the long run than those of the major recording labels. Only time will tell.

CHAPTER 4

Record Royalties

Money can be earned within the music industry in many ways. We're going to focus on the income earned from the sale of the finished recorded product; the performance of the recorded product on radio, television, movies, and the like; and from other methods in which record royalties are derived.

Record royalties are an area of negotiation within a record agreement whereby the artist provides services in the form of original recorded music, and in turn, the record company will be obligated to manufacture, distribute, promote, and market the artist's/band's recording to the public. In turn, the record company will pay the artist a royalty on the number of records sold. Based on this example, the definition, principal, and legal aspects of record royalties seems very simple. However, the negotiations of record royalties can be quite involved and convoluted.

Once the negotiation of royalties has begun between a band and the respective record label, the royalties must be defined within some parameters. Our royalties could be based on a percentage of the Manufacturers Suggested Retail Price (MSRP), or the royalties could be based on the manufacturer's wholesale price. For the purposes of our discussion, royalties will be based on retail price.

Several different calculations can exist during the negotiation of royalties for a band/artist. For example, if you are a new band/artist who has no proven record of accomplishment of sales, your royalty rates or percentage will not be as high as those acts that are well established. Generally, new acts can negotiate a rate of anywhere from 9% to 13%. Established acts in the music industry can negotiate royalties anywhere from 14% to 17%. In addition, of course, there are the superstars of the music industry who can command upward of 20% in record royalty negotiations. Some of you may be asking yourselves "twelve percent, fourteen percent, and twenty percent of what?" As mentioned previously, it is a percentage of MSRP or of the record company's set price for the sale of the album/CD. These rates generally apply to those record companies that are affiliated with the Majors.

As discussed in the record contract chapter, most contracts will contain option periods. If the band is successful and is selling CDs that are equal to or higher than the anticipated sales projections of the record company, they can earn higher royalties. The negotiation process in which this occurs is known as *escalating royalties.* Are royalty rates different for the CD than for a digital download? According to the Harry Fox Agency, the current statutory mechanical royalty rate for physical recordings, such as CDs and permanent digital downloads, is 9.1 cents for recordings of 5 minutes or less, and 1.75 cents per minute or fraction thereof for those over 5 minutes. Then this is multiplied by the number of recordings you wish to make. The Harry Fox Agency Webpage has a mechanical royalty calculator, which is a wonderful tool to use and understand how mechanical royalties are derived. As of the writing of this book, negotiations are underway to determine the royalty rate and the tracking and dissemination of digital downloads and digital audio and video streaming ... so things could change, and most likely will. I suggest you always keep abreast of the music industry by reading periodicals such as Billboard magazine and other music-industry periodicals.

So, can we say now that the calculation or negotiation of royalties is complete the band goes on the road and we're on our way to make The Big Bucks Deluxe? No, not quite yet. You knew I was going to say no, didn't you? Now we must delve into the minutiae of record royalty negotiations. We must discuss the fees and costs that are associated with the making of a recording. Then and only then will we truly know what the record royalty will be for the band/artist.

As mentioned previously, after the recording, mixing, and mastering of the original music, the master copy goes into mass production. Therefore, a customary deduction is made prior to calculating royalties, which covers CD inserts, art design, packaging costs, and more. Customarily, you should make certain that your entertainment attorney and artist manager negotiate this amount and have it delineated within the record contract. In today's economy, it's difficult to determine what these costs would be. In the past, say 10 to 15 years ago, these costs could run from 12% to 25%, depending on the complexity and depth of artwork created for the product.

Let's not forget ... Uncle Sam! What is it that Benjamin Franklin stated ..."In this world nothing is certain but death and taxes." Therefore, the accounting department within the record company will deduct all excise taxes and duties applicable to the recording.

Now the band/artist is ready to go out and show the world their musical prowess. Right? Not quite yet. The record company wants to ensure the band is going to get radio play. For the record company to accomplish this goal they give out hundreds of free CDs to the various radio stations across the country. These CDs are known as *Free Goods*. If you think about it, almost every new product that we purchase in stores or certain products online will initially be offered at a reduced rate or sometimes even free. Remember, "The first one's free." What they don't tell you is that the second one is going to cost you, and depending on the product that you're purchasing, well let's just say it could get quite expensive. Ahh, who am I kidding! Nothing is free these days! Oh, one important point not to forget, royalties are paid on CDs sold, not CDs ordered or shipped.

Based on the previous statement, if CDs are shipped but not purchased, what happens to them? Well, they are returned. Negotiations between record companies and the distributors that they work with vary greatly depending upon the amount of returns. It used to be that distributors would receive 100% of the wholesale price they paid for any product that they would return to the record company. Considering the economic status of our country and of the record industry as a whole, the negotiations on this point can be quite varied. I would suggest that your personal manager and entertainment attorney negotiate a clause within your record contract that states any returns could possibly be distributed through wholesale clubs, online, or in retail outlets. This is where you see the big bin inside your mega retail store with the CDs marked at $2.00 to $5.00.

Any artist manager needs to be aware of the fact that the band/artist will incur recording costs and other ancillary costs when recording their CD, including studio musicians, instrument rental, extended studio time, transportation, hotel, food, and many others. For example, when a record contract is negotiated, an advance of funds will be distributed to the band and their manager as a show of good faith by the record company that they believe in the marketing potential of the act they have just signed. An advance is a monetary figure that is calculated, again, by the success and track record of the artist/band. The biggest names have received *multi*-million-dollar advances in recent years. Now the unfortunate reality is when the artists receive their advance from the record company, they generally spend it on a number of things totally unrelated to the music industry, such as cars and jewelry. What the artist/band needs, I repeat, needs to do with the advance money is to pay for recording costs of their CD or pay off any existing debt they may owe. The record company can set up what's known as a *funds approach* in which monies are set aside for the recording project. If any funds remain after the project is complete, then that amount is disbursed to the artist or distributed equally among the band members. The method of *costs plus* may also be employed. This is where the record company will pay the actual recording costs and any additional funds that are required. The caveat to all of this is that ultimately all costs will be recouped by the record company from the band's/artist's royalties. So what does this tell you? It should tell you loud and clear that any funds you received as a band or artist prior to the release and sale of your product means you will not, I repeat, will not see a penny of royalties earned until your record company has recouped all costs. This is why we have all heard stories about many famous artists who have sold millions of CDs only to wind up bankrupt when everything is said and done. How can this be? How can an artist who sells millions of CDs wind up bankrupt, and have nothing to their name? I would suggest you investigate the following artists: MC Hammer; one of the highest-selling female groups of all times, TLC; Vanilla Ice; and many other artists and bands.

In the case that a band does not earn enough royalties from sales of their product to recoup the money owed to their record company, what happens? I hope that the artist manager has their act together enough to make certain this scenario does not occur! However, when costs for music videos, marketing, promotion, touring, recording, publishing, and a plethora of other costs that are associated with making a CD are calculated, the amount of money that is spent is staggering. So, back to our original question …"What happens if the band/artist does not make enough money to recoup costs?" The band/artist will then be subject to what is known as *Cross-Collateralization*. An artist/band will want to do everything in their power to avoid being placed in this position. Why? Because, *Cross-Collateralization* is the process of collecting debts owed by the artist/band to the record company until they are paid in full. This means that if the record company does not release you, and the band/artist releases another CD, no royalties will be earned by the band/artist until the debt from the first CD is paid off. Now don't forget not only does the artist/band owe from their first CD recording project, but they also owe the debt incurred for the new second album! And, heaven forbid they go into the red on their second CD release, then the debt owed will be for their first, second, and maybe a third record release. This has happened to many artists and bands. Moreover, if the artist/band is released from the original record company, and picked up by a different record company, they still cannot be paid any royalties earned until the debt owed to the original record company is paid for. What an ugly situation this can be!

Record producers' costs will also affect the amount of royalties paid to the band. The typical percentage that a record producer will earn for their professional insight when working with the band/artist can be 1% to 3%. Very high-profile record producers, such as Quincy Jones, Rick Rubin, and the like can command up to 5% of the royalties earned. Three percent is generally the amount that most record producers earn for working with a band/artist on a recording. In addition, not only can the producer be paid a percentage of the royalties earned, but they are also generally paid a flat fee for their services. I have seen it where the average flat-rate paid for services rendered was $50,000. There are producers today who do not earn that much, again, because of the economic structure of the music industry. However, the high-profile producers can command as much as $1 million and a percentage of the royalties earned. The percentage of the royalties earned are also known as *points* in the music industry. This is another negotiable item that should be discussed between the artist manager, the entertainment attorney, and the record company prior to any recording.

Xavier Frascogna Jr., and H. Lee Hetherington in their book, *This Business of Artist Management* put it best when they stated "Remember: It's Business." They are correct. Many individuals who have written music industry texts and have worked in the music industry for years in various positions will state, "The music industry is a relationship business!" This is something that you should all etch in your minds and never forget. The record industry is not about the quick kill monetarily, or at least it shouldn't be. I think the key to success in the record industry is longevity. Now I have my own thoughts concerning certain genres of music that can be approached using the methodology of the quick kill, meaning getting a one-hit wonder, negotiating the contract where you and/or the record company make 99% of everything, and the artist/band makes nothing. This happens quite frequently. However, for most of the artists that you have known of for a period of 10 or 15 years and longer are those artists whose management is smart enough to negotiate deals for their band/artist that centered on career longevity.

CHAPTER 5

Copyright

Copyright and copyright law. To capture the clearest understanding of copyright basics, let's go right to the source,<http://www.copyright.gov/>. Copyright basics: What is Copyright?

"Copyright is a form of protection provided by the laws of the United States (title 17, U.S. Code) to the authors of 'original works of authorship,' including literary, dramatic, musical, artistic, and certain other intellectual works. This protection is available to both published and unpublished works." Section 106 of the 1976 copyright act generally gives the owner of copyright the exclusive right to do and to authorize others to do the following:

- to reproduce the work in copies or phonorecords;
- to prepare derivative works based upon the work;
- to distribute copies or phonorecords of the work to the public by sale or other transfer of ownership, or by rental, lease, or lending;
- to perform the work publicly, in the case of literary, musical, dramatic, and choreographic works, pantomimes, and motion pictures and other audio-visual works;
- in the case of sound recordings, *to perform the work publicly by means of a digital audio transmission."

In addition, certain authors of works of visual arts have the rights of attribution and integrity as described in section 106A of the 1976 copyright act. It is illegal for anyone to violate any of the rights provided by the copyright law. These rights, however, are not unlimited in scope. Sections 107 through 121 of the 1976 copyright act establish limitations on these rights. In some cases, these limitations are specified exemptions from copyright liability. One major limitation is the doctrine of "fair use," which is given a statutory basis in section 107 of the 1976 copyright act. In other instances, the limitation takes the form of a "compulsory license" under which certain limited uses of copyrighted works are permitted upon payment of specified royalties and compliance with statutory conditions." (copyright.gov)

So what does the above statement mean? In relation to the music industry, original musical works are compositions that produce income. This income is in the form of mechanical royalties, which is paid for each recording sold and for public performances from these original works performed on radio and television, video games and movies, and even ring tones. Therefore, your original song or intellectual property is an important asset. This asset must be protected, and to protect it, you copyright the song and/or intellectual property.

Do not misconstrue the term "copyright" with "trademark" or "service mark." These legal parameters are very different and function differently from copyrights. When a band or an artist has written an original composition/song, legally speaking, once that song has been transferred to a tangible format; in this case a tangible format could be a piece of paper, a digital recorder, a linear tape recorder, even something as banal as a cocktail napkin, it could be construed as being legally copyrighted.

Copyright law was put into place to assist composers in the protection of their original intellectual property. Since copyright law began, it has been amended several times to accommodate new technologies and to modify and clarify principles of copyright. According to the United States Copyright Office, copyright grants specific rights to composers or creators of original intellectual property regarding their composition.

1.   The right of the composer to reproduce and make copies of their composition. Please pay careful attention that this says the "composer" has the right to reproduce and make copies of their composition, not an end-user or other individuals.
2.   The composer of their original composition has the right to distribute copies of said composition. It is important to note that once a single copy has been sold, the composition or compositions that are contained on the CD are now considered published works. You can perform your music in public without the work being construed as published. This is a very important point to remember because, once your work is considered published, anyone may request the right to perform and/or record your original compositions. Moreover, by law you must grant them the right to do so. This is known as a "compulsory license." I will discuss compulsory licensing further in this chapter.
3.   The right to make derivative works. The creator of the original material has the legal right to change it in any way he/she deems fit. In other words, they can change a verse, the chorus, lyrics, melody, etc., as they wish. No other artist/band has the legal right to do this unless they request permission to do so and license the changed song as a derivative work.
4.   The composer of the original work has the right to perform the song or songs in public.
5.   Lastly, the composer of the original work has the right to present their work in folios and sheet music.

If the above material is copyrighted, then what is not protected by copyright? According to the United States Copyright Office, works that have not been fixed in a tangible form of expression are not protected. Names, short phrases, titles (such as titles of songs), familiar symbols, and harmonic progressions or chord changes that are common within music, such as the Blues I-IV-V-I progression are not protected. Ideas, concepts, principles, procedures, methods, and the like are not protected by copyright.

Can the creator of an original composition transfer their copyrights or copyright to other persons or businesses? Yes, as long as there is a written contract that states the parameters of the transfer, and both parties sign it. Transfers are not the same as licenses. This means copyright owners can authorize

the use of one or more of their copyrights through licenses and if any violation of these rights occurs, the owner of the copyright may sue anyone who uses their creation without a license. These transfers should be recorded with the United States Copyright Office to establish a new record of ownership. A copyright may be bequeathed via a will, living trust, or other legal format depending on state laws. Under U.S. copyright law, "the copyright in a work referred to the author, if living, or if the author was not living, to other specified beneficiaries, provided a renewal claim was registered in the 28th year of the original term." What this means is that the copyright in works eligible for renewal on or after June 26, 1992, will vest in the name of the renewal claimant on the effective date of any renewal registration made during the 28th year of the original term. Otherwise, the renewal copyright will vest in the name of the party entitled to claim renewal as of December 31 of the 28th year.

Let's move on. How long does a copyright protecte your intellectual property/song or songs? There are two dates to be considered. One is for a work that was originally created on or after January 1, 1978. If your song was written or fixed in some type of tangible format on or after January 1, 1978, it is automatically protected from the moment of its creation. The length of protection is that of the lifetime of the author of the creation plus 70 years.

If your song or songs are "collaborative works," this means that you worked and created your song or songs with another songwriter, then the creative work is copyrighted for the lifetime of the last surviving author plus 70 years. So, for those of you who are out there creating many musical works and you're making some money from them, I hope that your success continues because it is a great way to take care of your grandkids and other family members.

A songwriter may be employed by someone and asked to create original music for a specific event or other creative work in some circumstances. A contractual agreement is then drawn up between the two of you and you have agreed to write music for another creative for a specific monetary amount; this is known as a work for hire. As far as copyright protection for this particular work, it is not the composer's responsibility to file the proper copyright forms, etc. The duration of copyright will be 95 years from publication or 120 years from creation, whichever is shorter.

There are tens of thousands of original works that were created before January 1, 1978 but were not published or registered by that date. What happens with these original works? If you or someone you know falls under this category, your works have been automatically brought under the statute and are given federal copyright protection, which is generally computed in the same way as for works created on or after January 1, 1978.

Before 1978, a copyright could be secured either on the date a creative work was published with the copyright notice or on the date of registration, if the work was in unpublished form. When copyright was first secured, the song was protected for a period of 28 years and an additional 47 years if the copyright was renewed in the 28th year. On June 26, 1992, an amendment to the 1976 copyright act provided automatic renewal of the term of copyrights that were secured between January 1, 1964 and December 31, 1977. Once a copyrighted work has run its full course of protection, what happens then? Can you have it copyrighted yet again by one of your family members? Was there an amended law that has been written into copyright law that automatically protects it for another 70-plus years?

No. The song or original composition now falls under the definition of public domain. What does public domain mean? Any composition that falls under public domain means that anyone has the right to use that song in live performance, musical recording, sheet music or folio, and any other format desired. I'm certain that all of you are extremely familiar with public domain pieces. This would be works by Mozart, Beethoven, Bach, and any other composer whose copyright for their original work has expired.

So how does a composer go about copyrighting their original material? Copyright registration is a legal formality intended to make a public record of the facts of a particular copyright. According to copyright law, "even though registration is not a requirement for protection, the copyright law provides several inducements or advantages to encourage copyright owners to make a registration." In the past, some composers would just have one or two witnesses in the same room to testify to the fact that they were the original composer. In other situations, it's been said that if the composer puts a copy of the music in an envelope in mails it to himself or herself via a registered letter through the United States post office, then the song or composition would be copyrighted as long as the letter was not opened. Long story short, don't do this. Even with witnesses in the room with you as you were composing your song, it is not a foolproof guarantee in a court of law that you were the composer of the original material. Any experienced entertainment attorney would tear apart both of those scenarios in court. Then what is the best way to go about ensuring your original composition is copyrighted? The United States Copyright Office has two forms that may be used to indicate a composition is copyrighted. For the purpose of musical compositions, form PA (known as the Performing Arts works form), is generally used for a composition that has both musical and lyrical content. The second type of form, form SR (known as the Sound Recordings form), is generally used for musical works without lyrics. These types of original compositions could include genres such as Jazz, Classical, Bluegrass, and many others.

It is recommended that composers of original works place proper copyright notice on anything they create. In this fashion, any of your original works seen or heard by others informs them that the work is original to the composer and indicates the year in which it was created.

The symbol © serves as notice that the original work is copyrighted. Also, the word "Copyright" is used. Generally, the original work's copyright notice would appear in this order: The first year of publication and the name of the owner of the copyright, and would appear as such: Copyright, or, © 2011 R. Reading.

The copyright forms may be obtained online through one of the performing-rights societies, the Harry Fox Agency, or the United States Copyright Office. Original works may be copyrighted individually, or as a collective work (in order to save money). For example, for an original composition with lyrics, you could fill out the PA form, which would include the name of the composer, the date of composition, the title of the composition, a recording of the composition, and a copy of the lyrics. You would also include your address and contact information should the copyright office desire to contact you. As of this date, to file a hard-copy copyright form, the cost would be $65. To file an online form, the cost is $35.

I would like to go back and discuss further the definition of compulsory licensing. Compulsory licensing means that once your song is copyrighted and published, you must

allow anyone who makes a request to use your original composition. Of course, a fee is associated with this licensing. Now when I'm teaching my class, I always use this Canadian band as an example, and all of the students go, "OOOOOO, we can't stand them!" The name of the group is Nickelback. Wow, I think I just heard you say the same thing. I'd like to present two scenarios to you and see which one you would deny or accept. Scenario one: You've written several original tunes, you are a successful artist, and the personal manager of the group Nickelback contacts you and asks if the band may record two of your songs on their upcoming album. Scenario two: You are a well-established guitarist, or bass player, or drummer, and the manager of the group Nickelback contacts you and asks you if you would be interested in touring and recording with the band. Now before you answer either one of these, I would like you to remember one very important statement that was made in the book, "The music industry is a relationship business!" So, based on that statement, what would your answer be to scenario one? A resounding "yes!" Or a vitriolic, "Are you kidding me?" How about scenario two? Same answers? I've asked this same question throughout the years to many classes, and much to my surprise, and I must say disappointment, most students answered they would not do it. If you fall under this category, please let me give you some food for thought. First, you are probably not recognizing the fact that you would be paid at least $5,000 to $7,000 per week just to perform. Trust me, I've been there and you are paid back and much more! Secondly, never—never, please allow me to say this one more time—never turn down the opportunity to perform or have your original compositions performed! Now, I do understand that there are certain moral conditions that may come into play. For example, I know that I would not want any of my original compositions performed by some Death Metal group ... maybe. I would have to speak with their management, with the group, find out what type of an arrangement they were planning to use with the song, and more. Maybe I'd be surprised and really enjoy what they've done to the piece. No matter what your reasoning may be, please, try your best to rid yourself of any musical prejudices. As these prejudices will do nothing but harm you in the music industry in the long run.

Let's discuss a few more terms and then I will move on to the various licensing agreements within the music industry. This next term is known as fair use. Fair use is used in a variety of applications by professionals, educators, and musicians who all state that fair use is a specified amount of time in which you may use any part of the original composition as long as it doesn't exceed—and this amount of time is generally used by most people who have made this statement to me—30 seconds. The common misconception of fair use is that you are allowed the use of copyrighted works without permission for critique, teaching, scholarship, research papers, and more.

So then, what is the period of time in which you may use a song for one of the reasons stated above, and have its use construed as legal? Thirty seconds, 20 seconds, 10 seconds, 1 minute ... well, how long? The answer is ... ZERO SECONDS! "Fair use" is a non-term. There really is no such thing as fair use in the music industry. Now I know many of you are thinking that we use music in school all the time and it's legal. You're right, it is legal. Because your school has purchased what is known as a blanket license from one of the performing-rights societies, or from a music publisher, which states that they have the right to perform said musical piece, one time, within the academic environment. That's it my friends, one time.

So, for those of you who are in certain classes in which you might be doing a digital media work, short film, or something that involves the use of a small excerpt of a piece that is currently copyrighted, if you use any portion of a copyrighted piece without first obtaining permission to do so, you are breaking copyright law. Particularly if you are using the copyrighted material for an assignment, a project, or any other format. Are there exceptions to this rule? Yes. For example, performance or display of a song by a non-profit institution or religious institution. However, you cannot make any type of recording or use the material outside of the educational or religious environment without permission of the copyright holder. In this day of illegal digital downloads, and peer-to-peer sharing, even the rule of thumb for fair use, as a one-time use for charitable, educational, or religious purposes without commercial exploitation, I personally think will not stand. Lawsuits abound for illegal downloads and the misuse of copyrighted material in the form of musical compositions, so do not take the risk and download songs from the Internet for anything, even if the site states it's for free. Your safest bet would be to contact an entertainment attorney and make certain you have obtained legal permission to use the composition prior to using it.

The reason I'm so adamant about this particular area of the music industry is that there is data that is coming out of countries such as England, the United States, Japan, Australia, and other large countries where they are losing tens of millions of dollars monthly due to illegal downloads. For those of you who do not agree with me, that is your right. But please do me one favor, after you've worked for many years in the industry and have created something that is near and dear to your heart and people begin to steal it for their personal use, let me know how you feel about that.

Let's move on to different royalty schemes. Record companies make money by selling CDs/sound recordings. The record companies pay composers and publishers royalties for the sales of the artist's/band's product based on the number of units paid for. The record companies then pay different types of royalties based on the usage of this intellectual property. Within the music industry, there are four, and if we consider foreign countries, five types of royalty schemes in which an artist/band may earn income. I would like to provide you a chart that shows the different types of royalty schemes and the division of income for each:

Types of Royalty Schemes: How songs generate income

Mechanical:	Paid by the record companies Collected by Music Publisher Pub.= 50% Writer = 50%
Performance:	Paid by Broadcast stations, nightclubs, other public forums: Collected by Performing Rights Society Pub. = 50% Writer = 50%
Synchronization:	Paid by Film and TV producers: Collected by Music Publisher Pub. = 50% Writer = 50%
Print:	Paid by Print publishing companies Collected by Music Publisher Pub: = 20% of retail price on sheet music; 10–12.5% on folios Writer = 8–12 cents on sheet music; 10% of wholesale price on folios
Foreign:	Paid by users of your song who are located in foreign territories Collected by Sub-Publisher: who retains 15%–25% as a fee before passing any earnings to a domestic publisher Pub. = 50% Writer = 50%

We discussed a variety of items under copyright law, the various legal parameters that are contained within, and the organizations that deal with these particular copyright issues. Let's delve into the agencies that deal with copyright as well as other issues of assigning rights for the use of songs and more.

ASCAP: THE AMERICAN SOCIETY OF COMPOSERS, AUTHORS, AND PUBLISHERS

All information derived from <www.ascap.com>

The only performing-rights organization in the U.S. owned and run by songwriters, composers, and music publishers.

What Is ASCAP?

The American Society of Composers, Authors, and Publishers (ASCAP) is a membership association of more than 410,000 U.S. composers, songwriters, lyricists, and music publishers of every kind of music. Through agreements with affiliated international societies, ASCAP also represents hundreds of thousands of music creators worldwide. ASCAP is the only U.S. performing-rights organization created and controlled by composers, songwriters, and music publishers, with a Board of Directors elected by and from the membership.

ASCAP protects the rights of its members by licensing and distributing royalties for the non-dramatic public performances of their copyrighted works. ASCAP's licensees encompass all who want to perform copyrighted music publicly. ASCAP makes giving and obtaining permission to perform music simple for both creators and users of music.

Who Is ASCAP?

ASCAP is its members—creative people who write the music and lyrics that enrich lives in every corner of the world.

ASCAP is home to the greatest names in American music, past and present—from Duke Ellington to Dave Matthews, George Gershwin to Stevie Wonder, Leonard Bernstein to Beyoncé, Marc Anthony to Alan Jackson, Henry Mancini to Howard Shore—as well as many thousands of writers in the earlier stages of their careers.

ASCAP represents every kind of music. ASCAP's repertory includes pop, rock, alternative, country, R&B, rap, hip-hop, Latin, film and television music, folk, roots and blues, jazz, gospel, Christian, New Age, theater and cabaret, dance, electronic, symphonic, concert, as well as many others—the entire musical spectrum.

ASCAP members are individuals who make their living writing music. As a society of composers, songwriters, lyricists, and music publishers, we know very well that there are many steps between creation and compensation; months, if not years, can pass between the creation of a song, its recording, its release, its performance, and the day when the revenues due to the writer actually arrive. A music creator is like a small business, and ASCAP exists to ensure that music creators are paid promptly when their works are performed publicly. Some of the many other ways in which ASCAP can help writers include workshops, showcases, our Website and publications, and an exclusive, tailor-made benefits package that includes health and instrument insurance, a credit union, discounts on musical accessories, travel, and much more. ASCAP is committed to nurturing music makers throughout their careers.

BMI: BROADCAST MUSIC, INC.

All information derived from <www.bmi.com>

Broadcast Music, Inc. (BMI) collects license fees on behalf of the more than 500,000 songwriters, composers, and music publishers it represents and distributes those fees as royalties to members whose works have been publicly performed.

As a performing-rights organization, or PRO, BMI issues licenses to various users of music, including television and radio stations and networks; new media, including Internet services and Websites, and mobile technology businesses such as ringtone and ringback providers; satellite audio services like XM and Sirius; nightclubs, discos, hotels, bars, restaurants, and other businesses; digital jukeboxes; and live concert venues.

BMI currently represents some more than 7.5 million compositions—a number that is constantly growing. As a result, BMI has, over the years, implemented a number of technological innovations in its continuing effort to gather the most accurate information available about where, when, and how its members' compositions are played or performed, as well as ensuring that royalty payments are made in as precise and timely a manner as possible.

SESAC: SOCIETY OF EUROPEAN STAGE AUTHORS AND COMPOSERS

All information derived from <www.sesac.com>

SESAC was founded in New York in 1930 by German immigrant Paul Heinecke in an effort to help European publishers with their American performance royalties. Throughout the decades, until his passing in 1972, Paul Heinecke guided SESAC with his own unique mix of old-world charm and twentieth-century savvy and built the organization on service, tradition, and innovation.

With an established cornerstone repertory of the finest European Classical Music, SESAC began to turn its attention to American music in the 1930s.

The company's tradition of service began in the '30s when SESAC helped broadcasters satisfy FCC requirements, supplying them with quality recordings of SESAC's substantial Gospel catalog. The stations got their much-needed music, and SESAC established enduring relationships with broadcasters across the nation.

The 1940s was a time of worldwide upheaval, but SESAC continued to grow and evolve throughout the decade, redefining itself as circumstances demanded. By decade's end, SESAC had managed not only to survive, but to considerably broaden its reach and its repertory.

The 1950s saw the explosion of the radio and pop music and the establishment of SESAC'S innovative electronic transcription series.

On a monthly basis, radio stations would receive another "transcription" of exclusive SESAC music performed by the likes of Duke Ellington, Count Basie, Woody Herman, Coleman Hawkins, Elliot Lawrence, Joe Venuti, Chico Hamilton, Jackie Wilson, Chet Atkins, and Hank Garland, to name a few.

"It's heartwarming to see the fruits of our combined efforts ... writers, publishers, producers, users. ... As to the future, we shall continue to use as our buckler and our shield the eternal qualities of faith and hope, knowing full well that these, coupled with diligent and honest effort, shall inure to the benefit of all."—Paul Heinecke in 1950, on the occasion of SESAC's 20th anniversary.

In the 1960s, SESAC took its first steps into the mainstream pop music market.

SESAC continued its steady growth during the '60s, moving into new midtown headquarters at the Coliseum in Manhattan's Columbus Circle and opening its first Nashville office (headed by country star Roy Drusky) in 1964.

The year 1970 marked a historic turning point for SESAC as the company signed its first-ever songwriter agreement. Prior to that time, SESAC signed only publishers. Also in the early '70s, SESAC began a new focus on its Christian roster, helping to pioneer the Contemporary Christian format.

SESAC continued to grow during the 1980s, particularly in Nashville, where the company moved its headquarters in 1985. SESAC focused on technology in the 1990s with the introduction of innovative technology in performance detection.

The SESAC repertory grew substantially during the decade across all genres, particularly in the areas of R&B/hip-hop, country, and rock. The purchase of SESAC by Stephen Swid, Allen & Co, Freddie Gershon, and Ira Smith in 1992 and the subsequent signing of Bob Dylan and Neil Diamond marked the beginning of a new era for the company. In the new century, SESAC turned its attention to film and television, music, affiliating some of Hollywood's top composers. With the establishment of a Los Angeles office in 2000, SESAC began affiliating television composers like Jonathan Wolff (*Seinfeld, Will & Grace, Less than Perfect, Reba*), Dennis Brown (*Still Standing, Two and a Half Men*), Danny Lux (*Boston Legal, The Bachelor, Medical Investigation*), Bruce Miller (*Becker, Frasier*), Jon Ehrlich (*The Guardian*), and film composers like John Swihart (*Napoleon Dynamite*) and Chris Beck (*Under The Tuscan Sun, A Cinderellas Story, Taxi*). SESAC's Latina operation was also moved from New York to LA to capitalize on the exploding Latin music scene on the West Coast.

In 2003, the company negotiated a historic agreement with the Television Music Licensing Committee (TMLC). Based upon SESAC's substantial increase in television market share, the TMLC increased SESAC's share of performing-rights revenue generated by local television. In 2004, SESAC's Senior VP Pat Collins rose to the position of President/COO. SESAC has continued to grow and today stands as the clear technological leader among the nation's performing-rights organizations, using cutting-edge technologies to provide its affiliates with incomparable accuracy and consistency in performance detection over any medium, including the Internet. SESAC represents such musical icons as Bob Dylan, Neil Diamond, Robert Johnson, RUSH, Cassandra Wilson, Bryan-Michael Cox, Nate "Danja" Hills, Jack Knight, Jason Perry, Swizz Beatz, as well as many others. Artists who have performed SESAC-affiliated compositions include Justin Timberlake, Mary J. Blige, Usher, Mariah Carey, Beyoncé, Reba McEntire, Pussycat Dolls, Nelly Furtado, U2, and Christina Aguilera.

Of the three performing-rights societies presented above, all have their advantages as to which one you would like to belong. An artist can belong to all three performing-rights societies if they and their personal management think that a specific song from their album will be better represented by one performing-rights society than the other. This is why you see a list of so many great artists with each performing-rights society, and you may find their name listed with more than one of the societies.

What happens when an artist's/band's copyrights are violated, wherein there is a deliberate copyright infringement? Once again, any time someone downloads, records, performs or uses any copyrighted song without the express written permission of the owner of the copyright, infringement has occurred. In order to prove copyright infringement, the copyright owner must establish these parameters:

1. That the creators of the original material are the owners of the copyright.
2. That the infringing song or songs are substantially similar to the original songs.
3. That the infringers had access to the creator's original music. (Rapaport)

There have been many cases of copyright infringement throughout the music industry dating back prior to the 1950s. A few examples are Ray Parker Jr. being sued by Huey Lewis and The News for Ray Parker Jr.'s song "Ghostbusters," which was a direct infringement upon the song "I Want a New Drug" by Huey Lewis and The News. Another famous infringement was that of the rapper Vanilla Ice and his misuse of the song by Freddie Mercury and David Bowie, "Under Pressure." And there are many others.

The legalities behind such infringements are described as Contributory Infringement and Vicarious Liability. For example, you know of an individual or individuals who are illegally downloading music online, or sampling parts of an original composition from a CD, you could be guilty of Contributory Infringement. For instance, you could be the individual who gave them the CDs from which to sample. Or directing your friends to an online site from which to illegally download music, then you are guilty of Contributory Infringement.

Secondly, if you downloaded copyrighted material and then provided access to your friends to this downloaded copyrighted material, then you would be guilty of Vicarious Liability. The caveat to Vicarious Liability is that you must benefit financially from the infringing activities.

THE HARRY FOX AGENCY

Information derived from <www.harryfox.com>

The Harry Fox Agency, commonly referred to as HFA, is the foremost mechanical licensing, collection, and distribution agency for music publishers in the United States. Their processes, culture, and technology are client-driven and results-oriented. They continually strive to add value and strength to the music-rights industry. In 1927, the National Music Publishers Association established HFA to act as an information source, clearinghouse, and monitoring service for licensing musical copyrights. Since its founding, HFA has provided efficient and convenient services for publishers, licensees, and a broad spectrum of music users.

With its current level of publisher representation, HFA licenses the largest percentage of the mechanical and digital uses of music in the United States on CDs, digital services, records, tapes and imported phonorecords.

Back in 1927, the majority of the money made in the music industry was that from music publishing and some from recorded music as well. Harry Fox assessed that the performing-rights societies no longer had the wherewithal to accurately track and administer the collection, administration, and distribution of mechanical—and at that time, synchronization—royalties. Harry Fox decided to start his own company that would offer the services for a nominal fee and assist the performing-rights societies in their collection and distribution of said royalties. As of 2002, HFA no longer collects or distributes synchronization royalties. If for some reason you ever needed information pertaining to publishers of certain musical acts/artists, one of the first places to contact would be the Harry Fox Agency.

Lastly, many organizations have been formed or were already in place and established regulations against copyright infringement.

The RIAA (Recording Industry Association of America) is such an organization, which pursues copyright infringement and piracy and prosecutes accordingly. The RIAA was a major player in the lawsuits against Napster, LimeWire, and other online providers of free music downloads. In 1998, the Digital Millennium Copyright Act made it a crime to circumvent antipiracy measures that are built into commercial software and CDs. Other organizations such as the IRMA (International Recording Media Association) were also established to help prevent unauthorized manufacturing and distribution of copyrighted materials.

The bottom line here is musicians work extremely hard, most of their lives, in the hopes that opportunity might knock and they have a chance at success within the music industry. This could be you some day. Begin now to give our talented artists in the industry their due, not only in appreciation of their music, but also in monetary compensation.

EXAMPLES OF COPYRIGHT PA AND SR FORMS:

 Form PA

Detach and read these instructions before completing this form.
Make sure all applicable spaces have been filled in before you return this form.

BASIC INFORMATION

When to Use This Form: Use Form PA for registration of published or unpublished works of the performing arts. This class includes works prepared for the purpose of being "performed" directly before an audience or indirectly "by means of any device or process." Works of the performing arts include: (1) musical works, including any accompanying words; (2) dramatic works, including any accompanying music; (3) pantomimes and choreographic works; and (4) motion pictures and other audiovisual works.

Deposit to Accompany Application: An application for copyright registration must be accompanied by a deposit consisting of copies or phonorecords representing the entire work for which registration is made. The following are the general deposit requirements as set forth in the statute:

Unpublished Work: Deposit one complete copy (or phonorecord).

Published Work: Deposit two complete copies (or one phonorecord) of the best edition.

Work First Published Outside the United States: Deposit one complete copy (or phonorecord) of the first foreign edition.

Contribution to a Collective Work: Deposit one complete copy (or phonorecord) of the best edition of the collective work.

Motion Pictures: Deposit *both* of the following: (1) a separate written description of the contents of the motion picture; and (2) for a published work, one complete copy of the best edition of the motion picture; or, for an unpublished work, one complete copy of the motion picture or identifying material. Identifying material may be either an audiorecording of the entire soundtrack or one frame enlargement or similar visual print from each 10-minute segment.

The Copyright Notice: Before March 1, 1989, the use of copyright notice was mandatory on all published works, and any work first published before that date should have carried a notice. For works first published on and after March 1, 1989, use of the copyright notice is optional. For more information about copyright notice, see Circular 3, *Copyright Notice.*

For Further Information: To speak to a Copyright Office staff member, call (202) 707-3000. Recorded information is available 24 hours a day. Order forms and other publications from the address in space 9 or call the Forms and Publications Hotline at (202) 707-9100. Access and download circulars, certain forms, and other information from the Copyright Office website at *www.copyright.gov.*

LINE-BY-LINE INSTRUCTIONS

Please type or print using black ink. The form is used to produce the certificate.

SPACE 1: Title

Title of This Work: Every work submitted for copyright registration must be given a title to identify that particular work. If the copies or phonorecords of the work bear a title (or an identifying phrase that could serve as a title), transcribe that wording *completely* and *exactly* on the application. Indexing of the registration and future identification of the work will depend on the information you give here. If the work you are registering is an entire "collective work" (such as a collection of plays or songs), give the overall title of the collection. If you are registering one or more individual contributions to a collective work, give the title of each contribution, followed by the title of the collection. For an unpublished collection, you may give the titles of the individual works after the collection title.

Previous or Alternative Titles: Complete this space if there are any additional titles for the work under which someone searching for the registration might be likely to look, or under which a document pertaining to the work might be recorded.

Nature of This Work: Briefly describe the general nature or character of the work being registered for copyright. Examples: "Music"; "Song Lyrics"; "Words and Music"; "Drama"; "Musical Play"; "Choreography"; "Pantomime"; "Motion Picture"; "Audiovisual Work."

SPACE 2: Author(s)

General Instructions: After reading these instructions, decide who are the "authors" of this work for copyright purposes. Then, unless the work is a "collective work," give the requested information about every "author" who contributed any appreciable amount of copyrightable matter to this version of the work. If you need further space, request additional Continuation Sheets. In the case of a collective work such as a songbook or a collection of plays, give information about the author of the collective work as a whole.

Name of Author: The fullest form of the author's name should be given. Unless the work was "made for hire," the individual who actually created the work is its "author." In the case of a work made for hire, the statute provides that "the employer or other person for whom the work was prepared is considered the author."

What Is a "Work Made for Hire"? A "work made for hire" is defined as: (1) "a work prepared by an employee within the scope of his or her employment"; or (2) "a work specially ordered or commissioned for use as a contribution to a collective work, as a part of a motion picture or other audiovisual work, as a translation, as a supplementary work, as a compilation, as an instructional text, as a test, as answer material for a test, or as an atlas, if the parties expressly agree in a written instrument signed by them that the work shall be considered a work made for hire." If you have checked "Yes" to indicate that the work was "made for hire," you must give the full legal name of the employer (or other person for whom the work was prepared). You may also include the name of the employee along with the name of the employer (for example: "Elster Music Co., employer for hire of John Ferguson").

"Anonymous" or "Pseudonymous" Work: An author's contribution to a work is "anonymous" if that author is not identified on the copies or phonorecords of the work. An author's contribution to a work is "pseudonymous" if that author is identified on the copies or phonorecords under a fictitious name. If the work is "anonymous" you may: (1) leave the line blank; or (2) state "anonymous" on the line; or (3) reveal the author's identity. If the work is "pseudonymous" you may: (1) leave the line blank; or (2) give the pseudonym and identify it as such (example: "Huntley Haverstock, pseudonym"); or (3) reveal the author's name, making clear which is the real name and which is the pseudonym (for example: "Judith Barton, whose pseudonym is Madeline Elster"). However, the citizenship or domicile of the author *must* be given in all cases.

Dates of Birth and Death: If the author is dead, the statute requires that the year of death be included in the application unless the work is anonymous or pseudonymous. The author's birth date is optional, but is useful as a form of identification. Leave this space blank if the author's contribution was a "work made for hire."

Author's Nationality or Domicile: Give the country of which the author is a citizen, or the country in which the author is domiciled. Nationality or domicile *must* be given in all cases.

Nature of Authorship: Give a brief general statement of the nature of this particular author's contribution to the work. Examples: "Words"; "Coauthor of Music"; "Words and Music"; "Arrangement"; "Coauthor of Book and Lyrics"; "Dramatization"; "Screen Play"; "Compilation and English Translation"; "Editorial Revisions."

SPACE 3: Creation and Publication

General Instructions: Do not confuse "creation" with "publication." Every application for copyright registration must state "the year in which creation of the work was completed." Give the date and nation of first publication only if the work has been published.

Creation: Under the statute, a work is "created" when it is fixed in a copy or phonorecord for the first time. Where a work has been prepared over a period of time, the part of the work existing in fixed form on a particular date constitutes the created work on that date. The date you give here should be the year in which the author completed the particular version for which registration is now being sought, even if other versions exist or if further changes or additions are planned.

Publication: The statute defines "publication" as "the distribution of copies or phonorecords of a work to the public by sale or other transfer of ownership, or by rental, lease, or lending"; a work is also "published" if there has been an "offering to distribute copies or phonorecords to a group of persons for purposes of further distribution, public performance, or public display." Give the full date (month, day, year) when, and the country where, publication first occurred. If first publication took place simultaneously in the United States and other countries, it is sufficient to state "U.S.A."

SPACE 4: Claimant(s)

Name(s) and Address(es) of Copyright Claimant(s): Give the name(s) and address(es) of the copyright claimant(s) in this work even if the claimant is the same as the author. Copyright in a work belongs initially to the author of the work (including, in the case of a work made for hire, the employer or other person for whom the work was prepared). The copyright claimant is either the author of the work or a person or organization to whom the copyright initially belonging to the author has been transferred.

Transfer: The statute provides that, if the copyright claimant is not the author, the application for registration must contain "a brief statement of how the claimant obtained ownership of the copyright." If any copyright claimant named in space 4 is not an author named in space 2, give a brief statement explaining how the claimant(s) obtained ownership of the copyright. Examples: "By written contract"; "Transfer of all rights by author"; "Assignment"; "By will." Do not attach transfer documents or other attachments or riders.

SPACE 5: Previous Registration

General Instructions: The questions in space 5 are intended to show whether an earlier registration has been made for this work and, if so, whether there is any basis for a new registration. As a general rule, only one basic copyright registration can be made for the same version of a particular work.

Same Version: If this version is substantially the same as the work covered by a previous registration, a second registration is not generally possible unless: (1) the work has been registered in unpublished form and a second registration is now being sought to cover this first published edition; or (2) someone other than the author is identified as copyright claimant in the earlier registration, and the author is now seeking registration in his or her own name. If either of these two exceptions applies, check the appropriate box and give the earlier registration number and date. Otherwise, do not submit Form PA; instead, write the Copyright Office.

for information about supplementary registration or recordation of transfers of copyright ownership.

Changed Version: If the work has been changed and you are now seeking registration to cover the additions or revisions, check the last box in space 5, give the earlier registration number and date, and complete both parts of space 6 in accordance with the instructions below.

Previous Registration Number and Date: If more than one previous registration has been made for the work, give the number and date of the latest registration.

SPACE 6: Derivative Work or Compilation

General Instructions: Complete space 6 if this work is a "changed version," "compilation," or "derivative work," and if it incorporates one or more earlier works that have already been published or registered for copyright or that have fallen into the public domain. A "compilation" is defined as "a work formed by the collection and assembling of preexisting materials or of data that are selected, coordinated, or arranged in such a way that the resulting work as a whole constitutes an original work of authorship." A "derivative work" is "a work based on one or more preexisting works." Examples of derivative works include musical arrangements, dramatizations, translations, abridgments, condensations, motion picture versions, or "any other form in which a work may be recast, transformed, or adapted." Derivative works also include works "consisting of editorial revisions, annotations, or other modifications" if these changes, as a whole, represent an original work of authorship.

Preexisting Material (space 6a): Complete this space *and* space 6b for derivative works. In this space identify the preexisting work that has been recast, transformed, or adapted. For example, the preexisting material might be: "French version of Hugo's 'Le Roi s'amuse.'" Do not complete this space for compilations.

Material Added to This Work (space 6b): Give a brief general statement of the *additional* new material covered by the copyright claim for which registration is sought. In the case of a derivative work, identify this new material. Examples: "Arrangement for piano and orchestra"; "Dramatization for television"; "New film version"; "Revisions throughout; Act III completely new." If the work is a compilation, give a brief general statement describing both the material that has been compiled *and* the compilation itself. Example: "Compilation of 19th Century Military Songs."

SPACE 7, 8, 9: Fee, Correspondence, Certification, Return Address

Deposit Account: If you maintain a Deposit Account in the Copyright Office, identify it in space 7a. Otherwise, leave the space blank and send the fee with your application and deposit.

Correspondence (space 7b): Give the name, address, area code, telephone number, fax number, and email address (if available) of the person to be consulted if correspondence about this application becomes necessary.

Certification (space 8): The application cannot be accepted unless it bears the date and the **handwritten signature** of the author or other copyright claimant, or of the owner of exclusive right(s), or of the duly authorized agent of the author, claimant, or owner of exclusive right(s).

Address for Return of Certificate (space 9): The address box must be completed legibly since the certificate will be returned in a window envelope.

MORE INFORMATION

How to Register a Recorded Work: If the musical or dramatic work that you are registering has been recorded (as a tape, disk, or cassette), you may choose either copyright application Form PA (Performing Arts) or Form SR (Sound Recordings), depending on the purpose of the registration.

Use Form PA to register the underlying musical composition or dramatic work. Form SR has been developed specifically to register a "sound recording" as defined by the Copyright Act — a work resulting from the "fixation of a series of sounds," separate and distinct from the underlying musical or dramatic work. Form SR should be used when the copyright claim is limited to the sound recording itself. (In one instance, Form SR may also be used to file for a copyright registration for both kinds of works — see (4) below.) Therefore:

(1) **File Form PA** if you are seeking to register the musical or dramatic work, not the "sound recording," even though what you deposit for copyright purposes may be in the form of a phonorecord.

(2) **File Form PA** if you are seeking to register the audio portion of an audiovisual work, such as a motion picture soundtrack; these are considered integral parts of the audiovisual work.

(3) **File Form SR** if you are seeking to register the "sound recording" itself, that is, the work that results from the fixation of a series of musical, spoken, or other sounds, but not the underlying musical or dramatic work.

(4) **File Form SR** if you are the copyright claimant for both the underlying musical or dramatic work and the sound recording, *and* you prefer to register both on the same form.

(5) **File both forms PA and SR** if the copyright claimant for the underlying work and sound recording differ, or you prefer to have separate registration for them.

"Copies" and "Phonorecords": To register for copyright, you are required to deposit "copies" or "phonorecords." These are defined as follows:

Musical compositions may be embodied (fixed) in "copies," objects from which a work can be read or visually perceived, directly or with the aid of a machine or device, such as manuscripts, books, sheet music, film, and videotape. They may also be fixed in "phonorecords," objects embodying fixations of sounds, such as tapes and phonograph disks, commonly known as phonograph records. For example, a song (the work to be registered) can be reproduced in sheet music ("copies") or phonograph records ("phonorecords"), or both.

Privacy Act Notice: Sections 408-410 of title 17 of the *United States Code* authorize the Copyright Office to collect the personally identifying information requested on this form in order to process the application for copyright registration. By providing this information you are agreeing to routine uses of the information that include publication to give legal notice of your copyright claim as required by 17 U.S.C. §705. It will appear in the Office's online catalog. If you do not provide the information requested, registration may be refused or delayed, and you may not be entitled to certain relief, remedies, and benefits under the copyright law.

Ⓒ Form PA
For a Work of Performing Arts
UNITED STATES COPYRIGHT OFFICE

REGISTRATION NUMBER

PA   PAU

EFFECTIVE DATE OF REGISTRATION

Month   Day   Year

DO NOT WRITE ABOVE THIS LINE. IF YOU NEED MORE SPACE, USE A SEPARATE CONTINUATION SHEET.

1

TITLE OF THIS WORK ▼

PREVIOUS OR ALTERNATIVE TITLES ▼

NATURE OF THIS WORK ▼ See instructions

2

a

NAME OF AUTHOR ▼

DATES OF BIRTH AND DEATH
Year Born ▼   Year Died ▼

Was this contribution to the work a "work made for hire"?
☐ Yes
☐ No

AUTHOR'S NATIONALITY OR DOMICILE
Name of Country
OR { Citizen of _____
      Domiciled in _____

WAS THIS AUTHOR'S CONTRIBUTION TO THE WORK
Anonymous?   ☐ Yes ☐ No
Pseudonymous?   ☐ Yes ☐ No

If the answer to either of these questions is "Yes," see detailed instructions.

NATURE OF AUTHORSHIP Briefly describe nature of material created by this author in which copyright is claimed. ▼

NOTE
Under the law, the "author" of a "work made for hire" is generally the employer, not the employee (see instructions). For any part of this work that was "made for hire" check "Yes" in the space provided, give the employer (or other person for whom the work was prepared) as "Author" of that part, and leave the space for dates of birth and death blank.

b

NAME OF AUTHOR ▼

DATES OF BIRTH AND DEATH
Year Born ▼   Year Died ▼

Was this contribution to the work a "work made for hire"?
☐ Yes
☐ No

AUTHOR'S NATIONALITY OR DOMICILE
Name of Country
OR { Citizen of _____
      Domiciled in _____

WAS THIS AUTHOR'S CONTRIBUTION TO THE WORK
Anonymous?   ☐ Yes ☐ No
Pseudonymous?   ☐ Yes ☐ No

If the answer to either of these questions is "Yes," see detailed instructions.

NATURE OF AUTHORSHIP Briefly describe nature of material created by this author in which copyright is claimed. ▼

c

NAME OF AUTHOR ▼

DATES OF BIRTH AND DEATH
Year Born ▼   Year Died ▼

Was this contribution to the work a "work made for hire"?
☐ Yes
☐ No

AUTHOR'S NATIONALITY OR DOMICILE
Name of Country
OR { Citizen of _____
      Domiciled in _____

WAS THIS AUTHOR'S CONTRIBUTION TO THE WORK
Anonymous?   ☐ Yes ☐ No
Pseudonymous?   ☐ Yes ☐ No

If the answer to either of these questions is "Yes," see detailed instructions.

NATURE OF AUTHORSHIP Briefly describe nature of material created by this author in which copyright is claimed. ▼

3

a YEAR IN WHICH CREATION OF THIS WORK WAS COMPLETED
_____ Year
This information must be given in all cases.

b DATE AND NATION OF FIRST PUBLICATION OF THIS PARTICULAR WORK
Complete this information ONLY if this work has been published.
Month _____ Day _____ Year _____
_____ Nation

4

See instructions before completing this space.

COPYRIGHT CLAIMANT(S) Name and address must be given even if the claimant is the same as the author given in space 2. ▼

TRANSFER If the claimant(s) named here in space 4 is (are) different from the author(s) named in space 2, give a brief statement of how the claimant(s) obtained ownership of the copyright. ▼

DO NOT WRITE HERE OFFICE USE ONLY

APPLICATION RECEIVED

ONE DEPOSIT RECEIVED

TWO DEPOSITS RECEIVED

FUNDS RECEIVED

MORE ON BACK ▶
• Complete all applicable spaces (numbers 5-9) on the reverse side of this page.
• See detailed instructions.   • Sign the form at line 8.

DO NOT WRITE HERE
Page 1 of _____ pages

EXAMINED BY	FORM PA
CHECKED BY	
☐ CORRESPONDENCE Yes	FOR COPYRIGHT OFFICE USE ONLY

DO NOT WRITE ABOVE THIS LINE. IF YOU NEED MORE SPACE, USE A SEPARATE CONTINUATION SHEET.

PREVIOUS REGISTRATION Has registration for this work, or for an earlier version of this work, already been made in the Copyright Office?

☐ **Yes** ☐ **No** If your answer is "Yes," why is another registration being sought? (Check appropriate box.) ▼ If your answer is No, do **not** check box A, B, or C.

a. ☐ This is the first published edition of a work previously registered in unpublished form.

b. ☐ This is the first application submitted by this author as copyright claimant.

c. ☐ This is a changed version of the work, as shown by space 6 on this application.

If your answer is "Yes," give: **Previous Registration Number** ▼   **Year of Registration** ▼

5

DERIVATIVE WORK OR COMPILATION Complete both space 6a and 6b for a derivative work; complete only 6b for a compilation.

Preexisting Material Identify any preexisting work or works that this work is based on or incorporates. ▼

Material Added to This Work Give a brief, general statement of the material that has been added to this work and in which copyright is claimed. ▼

a 6 b

See instructions before completing this space.

DEPOSIT ACCOUNT If the registration fee is to be charged to a Deposit Account established in the Copyright Office, give name and number of Account.

Name ▼   **Account Number** ▼

CORRESPONDENCE Give name and address to which correspondence about this application should be sent. Name/Address/Apt/City/State/Zip▼

a 7 b

Area code and daytime telephone number   (   )   Fax number   (   )

Email

CERTIFICATION* I, the undersigned, hereby certify that I am the

Check only one ▶
- ☐ author
- ☐ other copyright claimant
- ☐ owner of exclusive right(s)
- ☐ authorized agent of _____

Name of author or other copyright claimant, or owner of exclusive right(s) ▲

of the work identified in this application and that the statements made by me in this application are correct to the best of my knowledge.

8

Typed or printed name and date ▼ If this application gives a date of publication in space 3, do not sign and submit it before that date.

_____   **Date** _____

Handwritten signature (X) ▼

☞   x _____

Certificate will be mailed in window envelope to this address:	Name ▼	YOU MUST: • Complete all necessary spaces • Sign your application in space 8
		SEND ALL 3 ELEMENTS IN THE SAME PACKAGE:
	Number/Street/Apt ▼	1. Application form 2. Nonrefundable filing fee in check or money order payable to Register of Copyrights 3. Deposit material
	City/State/Zip ▼	MAIL TO: Library of Congress Copyright Office-PAD 101 Independence Avenue SE Washington, DC 20559-6230

9

*17 U.S.C. §506(e): Any person who knowingly makes a false representation of a material fact in the application for copyright registration provided for by section 409, or in any written statement filed in connection with the application, shall be fined not more than $2,500.

Form PA–Full   Rev: 02/2009   Print: 06/2010 — 50,000   Printed on recycled paper   U.S. Government Printing Office: 2010-357-993/80,085

United States •
Copyright Office
The Library of Congress

> "To promote the Progress of Science and useful Arts, by
> securing for limited Times to Authors and Inventors the
> exclusive Right to their respective Writings and Discoveries"
> (U.S. Constitution, Article 1 Section 8)

VERY IMPORTANT! PLEASE READ THIS PAGE:

This PDF document **Form SR** is exactly the same as the one that you can download from the US Copyright Office's website except that <u>this</u> particular electronic version of the **Form SR** document has been modified so that you can use your Adobe Acrobat Reader to fill-in the blanks right on your computer screen. And then you can print-off the completed form so that it will come out of your printer looking as if you had filled it in using a typewriter. But, of course, since you're doing in on your computer screen, it's much nicer and easier!

THE MODIFICATIONS TO THIS VERSION OF THE COPYRIGHT OFFICE'S FORM SR WHICH ALLOW YOU TO FILL-IN THE FORM ON YOUR ADOBE ACROBAT READER WERE <u>NOT</u> PERFORMED BY ANYONE IN THE US COPYRIGHT OFFICE. THEY WERE PERFORMED BY A PRIVATE PARTY. <u>PLEASE DO NOT CONTACT ANYONE AT THE US COPYRIGHT OFFICE</u> IF YOU HAVE A PROBLEM FILLING-IN THIS FORM USING THE ADOBE ACROBAT READER. INSTEAD, IF YOU HAVE THAT SORT OF PROBLEM, PLEASE CONTACT THE PRIVATE PARTY WHOSE NAME AND E-MAIL ADDRESS APPEAR BELOW. IF YOU HAVE A QUESTION ABOUT THE FORM ITSELF — A QUESTION THAT HAS NOTHING TO DO WITH FILLING IT IN ELECTRONICALLY, THEN PLEASE REFER <u>THOSE</u> KINDS OF QUESTIONS TO THE US COPYRIGHT OFFICE AT (202) 707-9100 OR SEND AN E-MAIL TO: copyinfo@loc.gov

If you have questions about or need help with the particulars of
filling-in this form using your Adobe Acrobat Reader, please contact:

Gregg L. DesElms
deselms@royal.net

If you are submitting this form <u>on or after July 1, 1999</u>, please consult the US Copyright office at (202) 707-3000 or go to the US Copyright Office's website at   http://www.loc.gov/copyright   and learn about the fee increases which may affect what it will cost you to properly submit this completed form! This is really important!

Specific information about the new fee increases are contained in the US Copyright Office's *Circular SL4* which may be obtain as a PDF document by pointing your web browser at: **http://lcweb.loc.gov/copyright/circs/sl4.pdf**

Information about fees in general are contained in the US Copyright Office's *Circular 4* which may be obtained as a PDF document by pointing your web browser at: **http://lcweb.loc.gov/copyright/circs/circ04.pdf**

If you find that you need more room than this *Form SR* provides, you may need to use the official *Continuation Form* which may be obtained from the US Copyright Office's website at: **http://lcweb.loc.gov/copyright/forms/formcon.pdf**

If you determine that you need to submit the US Copyright Office's official Cover Sheet with this Form SR, you may obtain it as a PDF document by pointing your web browser at: **http://lcweb.loc.gov/copyright/forms/formdoc.pdf**

If you would like any other US Copyright Office forms, point your browser at: **http://www.loc.gov/copyright/forms/**

NOTE: At the time of this writing, Gregg DesElms has only made the *Form SR* into an electronically-fillable form. If you also need an electronically filable *Continuation Form* or *Cover Sheet* (or any other form, for that matter), then please contact DesElms at the e-mail address shown above and request one. If he gets enough requests he'll probably create the form.

If you would like general Copyright Information, please consult any of the US Copyright Office's various web pages and official circulars by pointing your web browser at: **http://www.loc.gov/copyright/circs/**

IMPORTANT INFORMATION ABOUT PRINTING THIS FORM SR

This form should be printed head to head (top of page 2 is directly behind the top of page 1) using BOTH SIDES of a single sheet of paper. That means the you will first print page 4, then put it back into your printer and then pring page 5 on its back. Dot matrix printer copies of forms are not acceptable. Inkjet printed copies of the forms sometimes require enlarging if you use the Acrobat Reader's Shrink to Fit Page option during printing. Therefore, to achieve the best quality copies of this applications form, it is strongly recommended that you use a laser printer.

The forms submitted to the Copyright Office must be clear, legible, and on a good grade of 8.5-inch by 11-inch white paper.The quality of the copyright application forms submitted for registration directly affects the quality of the copyright registration certificate you receive. The Copyright Office produces completed registration certificates through an optical screening system that utilizes an image scanned from the original application submitted. As a result copyright applications submitted that are of poor print quality will negatively affect the copyright registration certificate you receive. For these reasons, the utmost effort should be made to submit the best quality application form possible (hence, another reason to use a laser printer).

☑ Application Form SR ☑

Detach and read these instructions before completing this form.
Make sure all applicable spaces have been filled in before you return this form.

BASIC INFORMATION

When to Use This Form: Use Form SR for copyright registration of published or unpublished sound recordings. It should be used when the copyright claim is limited to the sound recording itself, and it may also be used where the same copyright claimant is seeking simultaneous registration of the underlying musical, dramatic, or literary work embodied in the phonorecord.

With one exception, "sound recordings" are works that result from the fixation of a series of musical, spoken, or other sounds. The exception is for the audio portions of audiovisual works, such as a motion picture soundtrack or an audio cassette accompanying a filmstrip. These are considered a part of the audiovisual work as a whole.

Deposit to Accompany Application: An application for copyright registration of a sound recording must be accompanied by a deposit consisting of phonorecords representing the entire work for which registration is to be made.

Unpublished Work: Deposit one complete phonorecord.

Published Work: Deposit two complete phonorecords of the best edition, together with "any printed or other visually perceptible material" published with the phonorecords.

Work First Published Outside the United States: Deposit one complete phonorecord of the first foreign edition.

Contribution to a Collective Work: Deposit one complete phonorecord of the best edition of the collective work.

The Copyright Notice: For sound recordings first published on or after March 1, 1989, the law provides that a copyright notice in a specified form "may be placed on all publicly distributed phonorecords of the sound recording." Use of the copyright notice is the responsibility of the copyright owner and does not require advance permission from the Copyright Office. The required form of the notice for phonorecords of sound recordings consists of three elements: (1) the symbol "Ⓟ" (the letter "P" in a circle); (2) the year of first publication of the sound recording; and (3) the name of the owner of copyright. For example "Ⓟ 1997 XYZ Record Co." The notice is to be "placed on the surface of the phonorecord, or on the label or container, in such manner and location as to give reasonable notice of the claim of copyright." Notice was required under the 1976 Copyright Act. This requirement was eliminated when the United States adhered to the Berne Convention, effective March 1, 1989. Although works published without notice before that date could have entered the public domain in the United States, the Uruguay Round Agreements Act restores copyright in certain foreign works originally published without notice.

For information about notice requirements for works published before March 1, 1989, or other copyright information, write: Library of Congress, Copyright Office, Publications Section, LM-455, 101 Independence Avenue, S.E., Washington, D.C. 20559-6000.

LINE-BY-LINE INSTRUCTIONS

Please type or print neatly using black ink. The form is used to produce the certificate.

1 SPACE 1: Title

Title of This Work: Every work submitted for copyright registration must be given a title to identify that particular work. If the phonorecords or any accompanying printed material bear a title (or an identifying phrase that could serve as a title), transcribe that wording completely and exactly on the application. Indexing of the registration and future identification of the work may depend on the information you give here.

Previous, Alternative, or Contents Titles: Complete this space if there are any previous or alternative titles for the work under which someone searching for the registration might be likely to look, or under which a document pertaining to the work might be recorded. You may also give the individual contents titles, if any, in this space or you may use a Continuation Sheet. Circle the term that describes the titles given.

2 SPACE 2: Author(s)

General Instructions: After reading these instructions, decide who are the "authors" of this work for copyright purposes. Then, unless the work is a "collective work," give the requested information about every "author" who contributed any appreciable amount of copyrightable matter to this version of the work. If you need further space, request additional Continuation Sheets. In the case of a collective work such as a collection of previously published or registered sound recordings, give information about the author of the collective work as a whole. If you are submitting this Form SR to cover the recorded musical, dramatic, or literary work as well as the sound recording itself, it is important for space 2 to include full information about the various authors of all of the material covered by the copyright claim, making clear the nature of each author's contribution.

Name of Author: The fullest form of the author's name should be given. Unless the work was "made for hire," the individual who actually created the work is its "author." In the case of a work made for hire, the statute provides that "the employer or other person for whom the work was prepared is considered the author."

What is a "Work Made for Hire"? A "work made for hire" is defined as: (1) "a work prepared by an employee within the scope of his or her employment"; or (2) "a work specially ordered or commissioned for use as a contribution to a collective work, as a part of a motion picture or other audiovisual work, as a translation, as a supplementary work, as a compilation, as an instructional text, as a test, as answer material for a test, or as an atlas, if the parties expressly agree in a written instrument signed by them that the work shall be considered a work made for hire." If you have checked "Yes" to indicate that the work was "made for hire," you must give the full legal name of the employer (or other person for whom the work was prepared). You may also include the name of the employee along with the name of the employer (for example: "Elster Record Co., employer for hire of John Ferguson").

"Anonymous" or "Pseudonymous" Work: An author's contribution to a work is "anonymous" if that author is not identified on the copies or phonorecords of the work. An author's contribution to a work is "pseudonymous" if that author is identified on the copies or phonorecords under a fictitious name. If the work is "anonymous" you may: (1) leave the line blank; or (2) state "anonymous" on the line; or (3) reveal the author's identity. If the work is "pseudonymous" you may: (1) leave the line blank; or (2) give the pseudonym and identify it as such (for example: "Huntley Haverstock, pseudonym"); or (3) reveal the author's name, making clear which is the real name and which is the pseudonym (for example: "Judith Barton, whose pseudonym is Madeline Elster"). However, the citizenship or domicile of the author **must** be given in all cases.

Dates of Birth and Death: If the author is dead, the statute requires that the year of death be included in the application unless the work is anonymous or pseudonymous. The author's birth date is optional, but is useful as a form of identification. Leave this space blank if the author's contribution was a "work made for hire."

Author's Nationality or Domicile: Give the country in which the author is a citizen, or the country in which the author is domiciled. Nationality or domicile **must** be given in all cases.

Nature of Authorship: Sound recording authorship is the performance, sound production, or both, that is fixed in the recording deposited for registration. Describe this authorship in space 2 as "sound recording." If the claim also covers the underlying work(s), include the appropriate authorship terms for each author, for example, "words," "music," "arrangement of music," or "text."

Generally, for the claim to cover both the sound recording and the underlying work(s), every author should have contributed to both the sound recording **and** the underlying work(s). If the claim includes artwork or photographs, include the appropriate term in the statement of authorship.

SPACE 3: Creation and Publication

General Instructions: Do not confuse "creation" with "publication." Every application for copyright registration must state "the year in which creation of the work was completed." Give the date and nation of first publication only if the work has been published.

Creation: Under the statute, a work is "created" when it is fixed in a copy or phonorecord for the first time. Where a work has been prepared over a period of time, the part of the work existing in fixed form on a particular date constitutes the created work on that date. The date you give here should be the year in which the author completed the particular version for which registration is now being sought, even if other versions exist or if further changes or additions are planned.

Publication: The statute defines "publication" as "the distribution of copies or phonorecords of a work to the public by sale or other transfer of ownership, or by rental, lease, or lending"; a work is also "published" if there has been an "offering to distribute copies or phonorecords to a group of persons for purposes of further distribution, public performance, or public display." Give the full date (month, date, year) when, and the country where, publication first occurred. If first publication took place simultaneously in the United States and other countries, it is sufficient to state "U.S.A."

SPACE 4: Claimant(s)

Name(s) and Address(es) of Copyright Claimant(s): Give the name(s) and address(es) of the copyright claimant(s) in the work even if the claimant is the same as the author. Copyright in a work belongs initially to the author of the work (including, in the case of a work made for hire, the employer or other person for whom the work was prepared). The copyright claimant is either the author of the work or a person or organization to whom the copyright initially belonging to the author has been transferred.

Transfer: The statute provides that, if the copyright claimant is not the author, the application for registration must contain "a brief statement of how the claimant obtained ownership of the copyright." If any copyright claimant named in space 4a is not an author named in space 2, give a brief statement explaining how the claimant(s) obtained ownership of the copyright. Examples: "By written contract"; "Transfer of all rights by author"; "Assignment"; "By will." Do not attach transfer documents or other attachments or riders.

SPACE 5: Previous Registration

General Instructions: The questions in space 5 are intended to show whether an earlier registration has been made for this work and, if so, whether there is any basis for a new registration. As a rule, only one basic copyright registration can be made for the same version of a particular work.

Same Version: If this version is substantially the same as the work covered by a previous registration, a second registration is not generally possible unless: (1) the work has been registered in unpublished form and a second registration is now being sought to cover this first published edition; or (2) someone other than the author is identified as copyright claimant in the earlier registration and the author is now seeking registration in his or her own name. If either of these two exceptions apply, check the appropriate box and give the earlier registration number and date. Otherwise, do not submit Form SR. Instead, write the Copyright Office for information about supplementary registration or recordation of transfers of copyright ownership.

Changed Version: If the work has been changed, and you are now seeking registration to cover the additions or revisions, check the last box in space 5, give the earlier registration number and date, and complete both parts of space 6 in accordance with the instructions below.

Previous Registration Number and Date: If more than one previous registration has been made for the work, give the number and date of the latest registration.

SPACE 6: Derivative Work or Compilation

General Instructions: Complete space 6 if this work is a "changed version," "compilation," or "derivative work," and if it incorporates one or more earlier works that have already been published or registered for copyright, or that have fallen into the public domain, or sound recordings that were fixed before February 15, 1972. A "compilation" is defined as "a work formed by the collection and assembling of preexisting materials or of data that are selected, coordinated, or arranged in such a way that the resulting work as a whole constitutes an original work of authorship." A "derivative work" is "a work based on one or more preexisting works." Examples of derivative works include recordings reissued with substantial editorial revisions or abridgments of the recorded sounds, and recordings republished with new recorded material, or "any other form in which a work may be recast, transformed, or adapted." Derivative works also include works "consisting of editorial revisions, annotations, or other modifications" if these changes, as a whole, represent an original work of authorship.

Preexisting Material (space 6a): Complete this space **and** space 6b for derivative works. In this space identify the preexisting work that has been recast, transformed, or adapted. The preexisting work may be material that has been previously published, previously registered, or that is in the public domain. For example, the preexisting material might be: "1970 recording by Sperryville Symphony of Bach Double Concerto."

Material Added to This Work (space 6b): Give a brief, general statement of the **additional** new material covered by the copyright claim for which registration is sought. In the case of a derivative work, identify this new material. Examples: "Recorded performances on bands 1 and 3"; "Remixed sounds from original multitrack sound sources"; "New words, arrangement, and additional sounds." If the work is a compilation, give a brief, general statement describing both the material that has been compiled **and** the compilation itself. Example: "Compilation of 1938 Recordings by various swing bands."

SPACE 7, 8, 9: Fee, Correspondence, Certification, Return Address

Deposit Account: If you maintain a Deposit Account in the Copyright Office, identify it in space 7a. Otherwise, leave the space blank and send the filing fee with your application and deposit. (See space 8 on form.)

Correspondence (space 7b): This space should contain the name, address, area code, telephone number, fax number, and email address (if available) of the person to be consulted if correspondence about this application becomes necessary.

Certification (space 8): This application cannot be accepted unless it bears the date and the **handwritten signature** of the author or other copyright claimant, or of the owner of exclusive right(s), or of the duly authorized agent of the author, claimant, or owner of exclusive right(s).

Address for Return of Certificate (space 9): The address box must be completed legibly since the certificate will be returned in a window envelope.

MORE INFORMATION

"Works": "Works" are the basic subject matter of copyright; they are what authors create and copyright protects. The statute draws a sharp distinction between the "work" and "any material object in which the work is embodied."

"Copies" and "Phonorecords": These are the two types of material objects in which "works" are embodied. In general, **"copies"** are objects from which a work can be read or visually perceived, directly or with the aid of a machine or device, such as manuscripts, books, sheet music, film, and videotape. **"Phonorecords"** are objects embodying fixations of sounds, such as audio tapes and phonograph disks. For example, a song (the "work") can be reproduced in sheet music ("copies") or phonograph disks ("phonorecords"), or both.

"Sound Recordings": These are "works," not "copies" or "phonorecords." "Sound recordings" are "works that result from the fixation of a series of musical, spoken, or other sounds, but not including the sounds accompanying a motion picture or other audiovisual work." Example: When a record company issues a new release, the release will typically involve two distinct "works": the "musical work" that has been recorded, and the "sound recording" as a separate work in itself. The material objects that the record company sends out are "phonorecords": physical reproductions of both the "musical work" and the "sound recording."

Should You File More Than One Application? If your work consists of a recorded musical, dramatic, or literary work and if both that "work" and the sound recording as a separate "work" are eligible for registration, the application form you should file depends on the following:

File Only Form SR if: The copyright claimant is the same for both the musical, dramatic, or literary work and for the sound recording, and you are seeking a single registration to cover both of these "works."

File Only Form PA (or Form TX) if: You are seeking to register only the musical, dramatic, or literary work, not the sound recording. Form PA is appropriate for works of the performing arts; Form TX is for nondramatic literary works.

Separate Applications Should Be Filed on Form PA (or Form TX) and on Form SR if: (1) The copyright claimant for the musical, dramatic, or literary work is different from the copyright claimant for the sound recording; or (2) You prefer to have separate registrations for the musical, dramatic, or literary work and for the sound recording.

The fee is $20.00 effective through June 30, 1999. After that date, please write the Copyright Office, check the Copyright Office Website at http://www.loc.gov/copyright, or call (202) 707-3000 for the latest fee information.

FORM SR
For a Sound Recording
UNITED STATES COPYRIGHT OFFICE

REGISTRATION NUMBER

_____

SR _____ SRU _____

EFFECTIVE DATE OF REGISTRATION

_____

Month   Day   Year

DO NOT WRITE ABOVE THIS LINE. IF YOU NEED MORE SPACE, USE A SEPARATE CONTINUATION SHEET.

1

TITLE OF THIS WORK ▼

PREVIOUS, ALTERNATIVE, OR CONTENTS TITLES (CIRCLE ONE) ▼

2 a

NAME OF AUTHOR ▼

DATES OF BIRTH AND DEATH
Year Born ▼   Year Died ▼

Was this contribution to the work a "work made for hire"?
☐ Yes
☐ No

AUTHOR'S NATIONALITY OR DOMICILE
Name of Country
OR { Citizen of ▶ _____
Domiciled in ▶ _____

WAS THIS AUTHOR'S CONTRIBUTION TO THE WORK
Anonymous?   ☐ Yes ☐ No
Pseudonymous?   ☐ Yes ☐ No
If the answer to either of these questions is "Yes," see detailed instructions.

NATURE OF AUTHORSHIP Briefly describe nature of material created by this author in which copyright is claimed. ▼

NOTE

Under the law, the "author" of a "work made for hire" is generally the employer, not the employee (see instructions). For any part of this work that was "made for hire," check "Yes" in the space provided, give the employer (or other person for whom the work was prepared) as "Author" of that part, and leave the space for dates of birth and death blank.

b

NAME OF AUTHOR ▼

DATES OF BIRTH AND DEATH
Year Born ▼   Year Died ▼

Was this contribution to the work a "work made for hire"?
☐ Yes
☐ No

AUTHOR'S NATIONALITY OR DOMICILE
Name of Country
OR { Citizen of ▶ _____
Domiciled in ▶ _____

WAS THIS AUTHOR'S CONTRIBUTION TO THE WORK
Anonymous?   ☐ Yes ☐ No
Pseudonymous?   ☐ Yes ☐ No
If the answer to either of these questions is "Yes," see detailed instructions.

NATURE OF AUTHORSHIP Briefly describe nature of material created by this author in which copyright is claimed. ▼

c

NAME OF AUTHOR ▼

DATES OF BIRTH AND DEATH
Year Born ▼   Year Died ▼

Was this contribution to the work a "work made for hire"?
☐ Yes
☐ No

AUTHOR'S NATIONALITY OR DOMICILE
Name of Country
OR { Citizen of ▶ _____
Domiciled in ▶ _____

WAS THIS AUTHOR'S CONTRIBUTION TO THE WORK
Anonymous?   ☐ Yes ☐ No
Pseudonymous?   ☐ Yes ☐ No
If the answer to either of these questions is "Yes," see detailed instructions.

NATURE OF AUTHORSHIP Briefly describe nature of material created by this author in which copyright is claimed. ▼

3 a

YEAR IN WHICH CREATION OF THIS WORK WAS COMPLETED
_____ ◀Year This information must be given in all cases.

b **DATE AND NATION OF FIRST PUBLICATION OF THIS PARTICULAR WORK**
Complete this information ONLY if this work has been published.
Month ▶ _____ Day ▶ _____ Year ▶ _____
_____ ◀ Nation

4 a
See instructions before completing this space.

COPYRIGHT CLAIMANT(S) Name and address must be given even if the claimant is the same as the author given in space 2. ▼

APPLICATION RECEIVED

ONE DEPOSIT RECEIVED

TWO DEPOSITS RECEIVED

FUNDS RECEIVED

DO NOT WRITE HERE OFFICE USE ONLY

b **TRANSFER** If the claimant(s) named here in space 4 is (are) different from the author(s) named in space 2, give a brief statement of how the claimant(s) obtained ownership of the copyright. ▼

MORE ON BACK ▶ • Complete all applicable spaces (numbers 5-9) on the reverse side of this page.
• See detailed instructions.   • Sign the form at line 8.

DO NOT WRITE HERE
Page 1 of _____ pages

EXAMINED BY	FORM SR
CHECKED BY	
CORRESPONDENCE ☐ Yes	FOR COPYRIGHT OFFICE USE ONLY

DO NOT WRITE ABOVE THIS LINE. IF YOU NEED MORE SPACE, USE A SEPARATE CONTINUATION SHEET.

PREVIOUS REGISTRATION Has registration for this work, or for an earlier version of this work, already been made in the Copyright Office?

☐ Yes   ☐ No   If your answer is "Yes," why is another registration being sought? (Check appropriate box) ▼

a. ☐ This work was previously registered in unpublished form and now has been published for the first time.

b. ☐ This is the first application submitted by this author as copyright claimant.

c. ☐ This is a changed version of the work, as shown by space 6 on this application.

If your answer is "Yes," give: **Previous Registration Number** ▼   **Year of Registration** ▼

5

DERIVATIVE WORK OR COMPILATION

Preexisting Material Identify any preexisting work or works that this work is based on or incorporates. ▼

a

Material Added to This Work Give a brief, general statement of the material that has been added to this work and in which copyright is claimed. ▼

b

6

See instructions before completing this space.

DEPOSIT ACCOUNT If the registration fee is to be charged to a Deposit Account established in the Copyright Office, give name and number of Account.

  Name ▼   **Account Number** ▼

a

CORRESPONDENCE Give name and address to which correspondence about this application should be sent.   Name/Address/Apt/City/State/ZIP ▼

b

Area code and daytime telephone number ▶   Fax number ▶

Email ▶

7

CERTIFICATION* I, the undersigned, hereby certify that I am the

Check only one ▼

☐ author

☐ other copyright claimant

☐ owner of exclusive right(s)

☐ authorized agent of _____

Name of author or other copyright claimant, or owner of exclusive right(s) ▲

of the work identified in this application and that the statements made by me in this application are correct to the best of my knowledge.

Typed or printed name and date ▼ If this application gives a date of publication in space 3, do not sign and submit it before that date.

_____   Date ▶ _____

Handwritten signature ▼

☞   X _____

8

The fee is $20.00 effective through June 30, 1999. After that date, please write the Copyright Office, check the Copyright Office Website at http://www.loc.gov/copyright, or call (202) 707-3000 for the latest fee information.

Mail certificate to:	Name ▼	**YOU MUST:** • Complete all necessary spaces • Sign your application in space 8
Certificate will be mailed in window envelope	Number/Street/Apt ▼	**SEND ALL 3 ELEMENTS IN THE SAME PACKAGE:** 1. Application form 2. Nonrefundable filing fee in check or money order payable to *Register of Copyrights* 3. Deposit material
	City/State/ZIP ▼	**MAIL TO:** Library of Congress Copyright Office 101 Independence Avenue, S.E. Washington, D.C. 20559-6000

9

*17 U.S.C. § 506(e): Any person who knowingly makes a false representation of a material fact in the application for copyright registration provided for by section 409, or in any written statement filed in connection with the application, shall be fined not more than $2,500.

September 1997—60,000   ♺ PRINTED ON RECYCLED PAPER   ★U.S. GOVERNMENT PRINTING OFFICE: 1997–417-750/60,019

CHAPTER 6

Recording Studios

Recording studios are where the magic of making music happens, and it is here where the rubber hits the road as far as making music is concerned. Studios today range from large professional facilities, professionally designed with millions of dollars' worth of gear, to small portable systems based on a laptop computer and a small interface. We live in a time that can be called "the digital age" only from a technological standpoint, and artists have a vast array of tools and toys at affordable price points for creating their artistic musical work.

PROFESSIONAL STUDIOS

The professional recording studio is made up of one or more rooms that are acoustically designed to be able to capture the best possible sound and get that sound onto a recorded medium. These kinds of facilities require acoustic designers and advanced construction techniques in order to create the optimum environment for music, and for other delivery methods such as audio for video and computer games. Another design criterion is to make sure sound doesn't "leak" into other rooms for isolation purposes, as well as create a comfortable environment for the artist, engineer, and producer.

The professional studio will have a control room designed to be a critical listening environment. The control room also houses the centerpiece recording console, excellent loudspeakers, and various pieces of ancillary gear that serve to enhance recordings. Control rooms are designed to be completely isolated from sounds created in the studio. The size of control rooms varies according to the needs of the users as well as the construction budget of the studio. Building a proper control room can be quite expensive when everything is designed and constructed to the utmost detail. It is not uncommon for such control rooms to range in the millions of dollars by the time all of the equipment is installed. Professional control room design takes into consideration comfort as well as sound quality, and all control rooms have a unique sound to them. The trick with control rooms is to get used to how music sounds in them, and how recordings might "translate," meaning, if a particular song mix sounds great in the control room, it should sound just as great on the majority of home and car sound systems.

The recording console is the nerve center of the studio environment; it allows for all input signals and output signals to be controlled and switched, which enables the engineer to move audio signals around the studio with ease. Professional quality consoles can be quite expensive—again some cost over a million dollars! The console should be considered the engineer's "paintbrush," giving the engineer the ability to shape the sound of a recording into a desired finished product. The most common feature of a recording console is the volume fader—the slider control that allows for changes in volume. Large consoles will have 80 or more such faders, allowing the engineer to adjust volume on as many different sounds at the same time. Complex musical productions require such consoles. Consoles have other standard features, such as equalization for every channel. Equalization allows the engineer to alter the timbre of a sound coming through a channel, very similarly to the treble and bass controls on a car or home stereo system, although, the equalization areas on a professional console will be much more flexible, accurate, and expensive than those found on home systems. Through its electronics, consoles impart their own sonic characteristic on sounds coming through them. There are some older consoles that have become quite popular with engineers and producers because of the sound of the electronics. Such vintage consoles can be restored and used in professional facilities (usually for about the same price as a modern recording console). Sometimes such vintage consoles

are "parted out," selling individual components to those who want the console's unique sound but cannot afford to restore an entire one. Consoles may also be "virtual" where the device looks like a traditional console, yet it functions to simply control the flow of digital audio on a complex computer system called a digital audio workstation (DAW). In this case, the console itself does not have a "sound" since audio never passes through it.

Control rooms will typically have more than one set of speakers available, with large powerful speakers mounted into the front wall of the room. Although, most engineers today prefer the smaller, closer speakers, the large powerful speakers are great for getting people excited about a mix played back at loud listening levels and for making sure the low end (bass) of a recording sounds good, since the large speakers are better at reproducing bass. Loudspeakers, also called monitors, are extremely important in a studio setting. Studio speakers must be as "flat" as possible, which means neutral, and that no one particular frequency area (low, mid, or high) is emphasized or de-emphasized. Imagine if the speakers you were mixing though sounded like they do at your local electronics store. At the electronics store, they want to sell speakers so the low end will be turned up, so will the high end, leaving the middle frequencies alone or even reducing the mids. If one were to try to mix on such a system, the mix would turn out exactly opposite of the speaker system! This is because low end and high end would be super emphasized on the speakers, causing the engineer to actually reduce the low and high end on the mix so that the whole mix sounds balanced on the home speaker setup, leaving you with a mix that is all mids with too little low and high frequencies. A lot goes into making speakers for the studio setting and to get them as neutral as possible. Speaker location can also have a major effect on how they sound in a room. Many studios will also boast a surround speaker system made up of five really great monitor speakers plus a subwoofer, just like home theater systems are now. In surround, one can mix music, dialog, and sound effects for film and television since the delivery format is also in surround. Special care must be taken to put dialog in the center channel and to keep everything forward until a special effect comes through in surround, otherwise the audience's head moves away from the action on the screen.

A very important aspect of a studio is the headphone system and the headphones themselves. The headphone system is one that takes audio signals from the console and sends them to an amplifier and then to the headphones. Since the headphone system is what musicians have to listen through when recording and overdubbing, they are of prime importance. To make a good recording, musicians must be able to hear what other players are doing as well as what they are doing themselves. Today, many headphone systems use a system called "more me" mixers. In such a system, every headphone location has its own mixer, allowing the musician to create a balanced mix for himself. This way they can turn themselves up (more me) to be the loudest part of their headphone mix, or just be able to customize their own headphone mix. Such more-me systems are more expensive to build than straight-up headphone systems, but they make musicians more comfortable. Another technology used for the musicians in the studio is closed circuit video cameras and monitors. If monitors and a camera are on each musician's location, it allows for each musician to see the others very easily (without having to look through various windows).

The digital audio workstation (DAW) is both software and hardware that functions to allow for all phases of music production—recording, overdubbing, editing, mixing, and mastering. The DAW is arranged by tracks just like a traditional multi-track recorder. Each track allows for editing of the musical material on that particular track, keeping in mind that a track is a recording of a separate instrument. Mixing is also a function of the DAW, allowing the user to blend tracks together to create the perfect balance. The DAW also allows for signal processing (or effects) on each of the tracks, allowing for a complex mix to happen right "in the box," meaning in the computer itself. The DAW is now pretty much a staple of recording studios and most home and project studios. The DAWs are less expensive and more feature-packed than traditional multi-track tape machines. Avid's Pro Tools software and hardware is probably the most-used DAW. Pro Tools allows the user to have a relatively small system (a small audio interface) or a large system (many audio interfaces) using the same software for both large and small systems. Such a system allows its users to take a project back and forth from a professional studio to a home studio equipped with Pro Tools without losing any data or recorded tracks.

As previously mentioned the multi-track machine (whether DAW, analog, or digital) is featured prominently in control rooms—they offer means to store multi-track recordings. This can be in the form of multi-track tape, where 2-inch-wide tape holds 24 separate tracks (the "vintage" way of doing things), or this can be in the form of a DAW, which can hold an almost infinite number of separate tracks. Separate tracks are important since they allow the engineer to control each track independently from the other tracks. If one track had a vocal and another a bass guitar, the engineer might want the vocal to be louder without affecting the level of the bass, for example. The console and the multi-track storage method form the heart of the equipment used in the control room and work to make studios unique from one another. We should probably mention the idea of analog versus digital here. Analog audio is recorded on magnetic tape where digital audio is recorded on a hard drive usually. Digital audio is made up of binary numbers that represent the audio waveform with excellent precision and fidelity. Digital audio is a relatively inexpensive solution for multi-track and 2-track stereo storage. Analog audio works by having magnetism fluctuate on analog tape. Analog tape is a less accurate way of recording. Generally, engineers and producers prefer the sound of analog tape, even though it is not as high fidelity as digital audio. Analog audio tape machines require constant maintenance and adjustment, but studios still have them for the sound they create when recording music.

Studios that are not completely based on a DAW platform will also have "outboard" equipment close at hand. Such equipment functions to enhance sounds in some specific way, such as equalization (perhaps more accurately than the equalizers on the console), and dynamic processing—adjusting the loudness/softness of an audio signal, or reverberation—adding the sound of an acoustic space to a recording. This equipment is typically arranged in racks behind or beside the listening position so that they are in easy reach for the engineer. There are certain staples of audio gear that a professional facility will have in those racks just because engineers like to use them. Some examples are the La2a compressor, the 1176 compressor, and Neve or API Equalizers pulled from a vintage console. This type of equipment (especially the Neve) has appreciated in value over the years, driving up their expense significantly.

Professional studio rooms are designed to be excellent performance spaces with acoustics that enhance sound created in them. Usually there will be a few separate rooms in the studio area designed to be acoustically isolated from each other. The size of the rooms depends on the type of music to be performed. Studios designed to record large ensembles will have the largest spaces, capable of holding an 80-piece orchestra, for example. Studios designed for commercial music recording will have a number of smaller isolated rooms each with windows giving musicians who are playing simultaneously the ability to see other musicians. Again, such rooms are designed to make sure sound from one room only minimally leaks into another room—this way an engineer can have separate control over each performed sound. Older-style studios (from the 70s and early 80s) use rooms designed to have minimal reflections, or in other words, to be acoustically dead. With this kind of studio, the engineer would add artificial reverberation. Newer-style rooms are designed to be more reverberant yet still acoustically controlled. This gives the engineer the ability to record natural room acoustics along with the main sound to be recorded. One interesting feature to note is that in most professionally designed studios, there are no parallel walls to be found—this is purposeful in order to reduce a particular kind of sound reflection in the room called standing waves.

Professional facilities will also have a large selection of microphones for engineers and producers to choose from. If the engineer is a painter with the console the canvas, the microphones would be the individual colors. The engineer knows intimately what each microphone sounds like and uses them to create individual sounds for instruments and vocals. Microphones also range in cost from a few hundred dollars to ten thousand dollars each for restored vintage mics. Microphone choice can make the difference when choosing a studio—many engineers are simply used to recording with particular microphones and will check to see if the particular studio has them before booking. Some of the staple microphones are the Neumann U-47 and the AKG C-12, which are vintage microphones usually needing restoration by a microphone specialist in order to function properly. On the other end of the spectrum would be the Shure SM-57, an inexpensive microphone designed for very loud sound sources, like drums and guitar amplifiers turned up to eleven. Gear choice is paramount to a recording studio's bottom line—equipment can be quite the investment, but also required in order to bring business in the door.

Whenever I walk into a studio for the first time, there are a few things I like to do. I like to look at the light fixtures to see if any light bulbs need to be replaced. I also take a peek at the bathroom and see how clean it is. Both of these things tell me much about how meticulously the studio keeps its gear. If the studio minds the details on things like their light bulbs and their bathroom cleanliness, then I can guess they keep their audio gear in the same shape. Second, I like to go into the control room and play some of my CDs through the various speaker systems. Recordings that I know very well allow me to check the speaker systems against what I'm used to hearing from my CDs on systems that I know well. This is called "critical listening." I will listen to the amount of low end the studio speakers are putting out, I'll listen to the amount of high end or high frequency information the speakers are giving out, and I'll listen to how loud the vocal is compared to everything else. These cues give me an idea of what I will have to listen for, as far as mixing and recording on the studio speakers, to make music sound right on any home or car speaker system. Studios are all too happy to let people come in and check their systems out because it could mean more business for them. The next thing to check out is the microphone list to see if they have the microphones I prefer, and just as important, how they store them. Expensive microphones placed on closet shelves with no protection for dust and particles that could get on the diaphragms is a sign that the studio doesn't take care of their mics. Microphones should at least be individually covered or, even better, stored in their own wooden boxes lined with felt or foam. Another item to check, if possible, is the wiring of the studio. This can be difficult because many professional studios run wiring under the floor or through the walls. Usually, however, you can check the back of the equipment racks or the back of the console and see if the wiring is neat and well kept. A studio is only as good as its weakest link and its wiring. Another check is to push up all the faders as well as the master faders to their max level and see what that sounds like. There should be a very even "shhhhhhh" sound coming from the speakers, without extraneous noises or buzzes coming through.

Many studios, both large and small, will have a lounge area with televisions, couches, perhaps a pool table, and well-stocked kitchens for between-session snacking, all as part of the service offered by the studio. Given two comparatively priced studios, the one with more amenities wins out. Clients need to eat of course, and many times they are working for over 12 hours a day, so it makes sense to offer some of the comforts of home.

The studio business has forever changed because of the number of so many project studios, audio for video/film studios, and multimedia studios. These kinds of facilities are smaller, much less expensive to build, and can rival the professional studio in terms of equipment and final result. Such studios reduce the need for the producer to record an entire project in a large professional facility. Instead, a music project can go to the professional facility only when one is needed for the room acoustics, microphones, or the critical-listening control room. For example, a producer might arrange to use a professional facility to record a large string ensemble for a particular song, and then continue to work in the project studio. When the project's recording stage is completely finished, the producer might then bring the project into the professional control room in order to mix under the best acoustic conditions. Large professional facilities have had to adapt the way they do business, as clients are moving back and forth between project studios and the professional facilities. Professional facilities that did not adapt largely have gone out of business. Also, the need for audio for video has dramatically increased with all the cable channels now available and screaming for content. Audio is also featured more prominently in home theater systems based on Blu-ray and DVD formats, which require high standards of audio production. Much of this kind of production happens in smaller studios now, and, budget permitting, the project studio producers are able to use large professional facilities sparingly and when needed. For the professional facility, this simply means that the client base must be much broader to cater to the needs of project studio producers, and still have enough business coming through the door to stay afloat.

PROJECT STUDIOS

The advent of inexpensive and powerful computer technology as well as music-making software (DAWs again) have made it possible for artists, engineers, and producers to afford project studios. The project studio ranges from a corner in a bedroom to a dedicated outbuilding, and by their nature cost much less than commercial professional facilities. The key to project studios is that given the right situation, they are capable of the same quality sound as their professional counterparts. Project studios are much more convenient—artists can work whenever they are inspired rather than booking a commercial facility in advance. Many artists will use their advance to purchase a home studio for their first recording, then upon the next recording, they can pocket the money that would have been used for recording costs.

A home project studio will probably not have a control room as acoustically well designed as a professional facility. This can lead to a number of problems, especially when it comes to monitoring or listening on the control room speakers. The project studio may not have the same quality critical-listening environment that the professional facilities have. Therefore, the project studio user might want to mix their recording in the critical environment after having recorded everything at home. Furthermore, a professional studio's rooms might be beneficial to recordings that would need a large well-designed room, such as a string section or big powerful drums. A recording might start in a large facility for initial recording then move to the project studio for recording everything else, then back to the large studio for mixing. This way of working can drastically reduce production costs.

With the advent of cable and the Internet screaming for content, the demand for audio for video has drastically increased, and commercial audio facilities can provide service to local, national, and international broadcast industry. (Not to mention that broadcasters and video content producers generally have bigger budgets than music-only projects.) Because of much-improved audio-delivery systems for video such as DVD, surround, Blu-ray, etc., much more consideration is given to audio quality, and this area is where the large professional facility can garner business.

Multimedia content is also in big demand especially for games. Imagine all of the professional audio production that was needed for game titles such as "Rock Band" and "Guitar Hero," and really every other popular home video game. Music and audio recording is vital for these products.

Since recording costs can be prohibitive to the average musician, some studios will rent their rooms out on "spec," which means on speculation. On-spec recording would be where the studio rents their spaces for no money or perhaps half of their normal full rate, with the promise of attaching to the artist's back end. This means the studio would get a piece of the recording artist's recording royalty until the full balance for the studio was paid in full. There is a saying that goes along with on-spec recording, which is "spec not to get paid"—either way it is a way of getting business from artists that the studio might not normally get.

Another aspect of the studio business now is to offer other full services, such as disc duplication, graphic arts for the covers, and even distribution from the studio's own record label. These are other ways recording studios can try to maximize their revenue.

Certain publishers have their own project studios, sometimes even a professional studio (like Sony in Nashville). These are used to make demo recordings for the publisher's writers. It should be noted that demo recordings today are much different from and much better than demo recordings of the past. There is no such thing as poor quality demos any more. The days of a demo being a "guy and his guitar" recorded poorly and just good enough to hear the song are over. Now, demo recordings are either almost as good or just as good as professional recordings, without apologies. Some of the publisher-run studios will also have an engineer as well as a studio manager booking time for the facility. Even though they are run by a publisher, such project studios will still levy an hourly or daily charge for using them, especially if an outside user has booked the studio as opposed to one of the writers.

We should mention something about mastering studios here. Mastering studios are usually separate from recording studios and have their own set of features that differ from recording studios. Firstly, the mastering studio has playback equipment and loudspeakers that are the very best quality, more so than what you would find in a typical recording studio. It is not unheard of for mastering studios to use loudspeakers costing over ten thousand dollars apiece. Secondly, the mastering environment is set up to perform as the very optimum listening environment—something most studios cannot duplicate just because of the size of the console and the fact that the control room has to have so much other gear in it. During mastering, the entire album is examined as a whole. Mastering serves to make sure that there is a consistent sound from song to song on the album. While mastering, special consideration is given to equalization and dynamic processing called compression. Compression serves to make the CD seem louder even though there is a maximum amount of volume for the CD format. If you notice on your own CDs, some play louder than others—this is a function of compression. After each song has been equalized and compressed, mastering involves sequencing the album, or determining the order of songs. Lastly, mastering involves getting a "master" of the recording—the source media that will be used to create all the copies when the project goes to a replicator.

STUDIO STAFF/PERSONNEL

The staff of a professional studio is the most important aspect of a functioning studio business. Generally there is a studio owner, engineers, assistant engineers, a studio manager, and various support staff. The staff engineers usually come with the studio rental and work with clients as engineers for their projects. Such engineers have complete command, control, and know-how of the studio system they are working with. Clients need only ask once for something and the engineer would get it done quickly and efficiently. Most audio engineers will have a background in electronics or music technology. Staff engineers have usually worked their way into the position by assisting for a number of years or they have come from another facility (along with their regular clients). Engineers are adept at translating the general request of a musician or producer into a technical procedure to be performed in the studio. Most producers and musicians are able to rely on the engineers' well-tuned ears to make judgment calls about the recording process and the recording, especially since they spend their time working in the same facility constantly. Engineers also tend to be good at troubleshooting problems that may arise with equipment and getting problems solved quickly enough so that the session doesn't come to a grinding halt. The engineer must be level-headed and have a smooth "bedside manner" in order to cope with the pressures of studio work and should be able to interact with people very well, as opposed to the "mad scientist" type who may be brilliant but can't connect with people. If an independent engineer is working in the facility, the staff engineer functions in an assistant engineer role, answering any questions and generally helping the independent engineer find his way around the studio.

The assistant engineer's duty is to assist clients with their needs in the studio. This can involve a variety of things such as setting up microphones and tearing down when the session is over, helping the engineer run down any problems that arise, or helping the engineer with complex systems such as console automation or the digital audio workstation. Some studios will furnish only an assistant engineer who is there to help, but not there to engineer the session, which would be the client's responsibility. Both assistant engineers and staff engineers put in many hours per week at a busy studio, and when sessions are not booked, are involved in maintaining all of the various systems used in the studio.

Studio interns or those wanting to become an assistant engineer will tend to work in client services first. Client service means attending to the clients' needs outside of the studio—everything from running to get food for everyone to helping musicians carry gear into and out of the studio to cleaning the bathrooms. Client services people are always on hand and ready to jump in when needed. Interns who are really good will perform such tasks even before they are asked to do so—this is a great way of becoming useful to the studio environment and subsequently getting hired upon completing an internship. During down times, the enterprising client services personnel will also try to learn as much as possible from the assistant and staff engineers about running sessions so if and when the time comes, he will be able to jump into the new role.

The studio manager's job is to take care of scheduling the studio and accounting and billing operations. Many times the owner will function as the studio manager since the entire facility is his investment. The studio manager must do payroll and payroll taxes and take care of the studio's physical needs just as one would take care of their own home. There are countless studio managers who spend their time with air conditioning companies and construction companies and even plumbers, since these are all part of the business ownership. The studio manager usually makes the schedule for the week that determines when the various engineers and assistants will work. Also, the studio manager is the face of the business giving tours to whoever might be interested in the studio, and constantly on the phone trying to drum up business. If the owner does not function as the studio manager, then the studio manger will keep in constant touch with the owner about everything going on or not going on in the facility. Lastly, it is the studio manager who hires and fires engineers, assistant engineers, and client services personnel.

Administrative staff might also be employed to take care of incoming calls and greet people as they come in the door. They should also have a copy of the studio schedule in front of them so they can answer questions about availability. Administrative personnel might also do double duty as client services (see above).

The maintenance engineer is a vital part of the team. Many studios cannot afford to have a dedicated maintenance engineer, opting to hire them as needed. Generally, the studios that have a maintenance engineer on staff will have the best-running equipment. Maintenance engineers troubleshoot and fix malfunctioning audio gear for the studio. With so many different systems existing in the same place, something is bound to need repair. Also, the maintenance engineer can modify gear to make it work better for the studio needs. Freelance maintenance engineers are expensive and called only when needed, usually staying on call at all hours since sessions can grind to a halt at any time because of equipment malfunction.

The producer and the artist are not a part of the studio staff; rather the producer and the artist are the client of the studio, and as the client, the producer and artist will dictate the production process.

Usually the producer dictates what will happen and when parts of the production process will happen. It becomes the job of the entire studio staff to make sure the client's needs are taken care of quickly, and to keep the producer and artist happy.

The mix engineer could also be a client of a recording studio. Mix engineers are usually independent (freelance) and specialize in mixing music as well as music for picture (video, film, multimedia, etc.) Mixing engineers are often able to charge significant rates for their services, especially when they have a string of hit records to their credit. If that is the case, labels, producers, and artists will seek them out to mix their hit songs hoping to capture the mojo that the mix engineer brought to previous recordings. Many mix engineers prefer to operate out of one studio they know very well, and producers and labels will send them the media to mix from, be it a hard drive or analog tape. Mixing engineers come from a variety of backgrounds, sometimes musical, sometimes technical, and sometimes just coming up through the ranks at a particular studio and turning independent. Most of all it is their ears, the ability to hear what a mix should sound like in advance. Then mixers work with the studio gear to make the mix happen. Talented and busy mixers will often have a production assistant (much like a producer) who assists them or who does the grunt work prior to the mix engineer's arrival at the studio. It is also not uncommon for mixing engineers to specialize in a particular genre of music, whether it is rock, pop, urban, etc., and become known for their success in that genre.

The project studio will not have all of the aforementioned staff; rather the project studio owner will most likely function as all of the above. Usually the project studio owner is also the engineer on projects that involve outside clients coming in, especially if the project studio is in the owner's home. It should be noted that there may be tax advantages from a home studio in the same way a home office would have such advantages—it is best to consult with a qualified tax advisor or CPA about such things. Wouldn't it be great to be able to write off all of your musical instruments and gear?

The phases of music production are as follows:

Pre-Production—the planning stage of music production. Producers and artists will usually work together on writing songs (or choosing them) as well as rehearsals.

Recording—This would be where the recording is taking place. After basic tracks are recorded, overdubbing takes place, which is where musicians listen to previously recorded tracks and add new ones.

Editing—this phase of production involves "cleaning up" tracks by deleting material that will not be used, as well as wholesale editing of sections of the song.

Mixing—During this phase, all tracks are played back and balanced by the engineer. Also special effects and other signal processing are added to create the sonic landscape.

Mastering—The final phase, where last tweaks and corrections are applied, as well as sequencing songs on the recording. Lastly, a master of the recording is made that goes to the replication facility.

These processes are explained further in the chapter on producers and the production process.

The Audio Engineering Society (AES) and The Society of Professional Audio Services (SPARS) are professional organizations holding annual conferences, giving technical papers and issuing standards used by audio designers and manufacturers. Students interested in audio engineering should become involved with these organizations, as both have educational programs, not to mention provide a central location for available internships. The Society of Motion Picture and Television Engineers

(SMPTE) is another professional group that holds conferences and issues standards that include audio engineering for video and film.

CHAPTER 7

The Producer and the Production Process

On many occasions, students have indicated they intend to become a producer when finished with their university studies. However, they don't necessarily understand that one common thread with producers is that they have already achieved success in some aspect of the music industry, and artists and labels want to draw upon that experience and success to make a recording with the producer. Becoming a professional producer is not an impossible task; it simply takes paying your dues. Since making a recording can be quite expensive, labels and artists are more apt to trust a producer with a proven track record and a proven method of working rather than a complete newbie. On the other hand, a new band with a new sound brought about by a new producer is often just what the industry needs to be turned on its ear. I realize that what you just read was contradictory—experience versus everything new (new act, new sound, new producer) but that is just the way it is. The best advice the future producers in the world could get is if you want to be a producer, go and produce a recording and get your experience built up. Take a chance on an unknown artist, come up with the money needed for studio costs, and when it is finished, try to shop your production to record labels. There is no better time than the present, although, you may want to finish reading this book first.

WHAT PRODUCERS DO

First and foremost a producer has to locate and join up with talent that has star potential even though the concept of discovering star talent can be a roll of the dice, at best. New star talent is always what those in the recording industry are looking for. Labels also discover talent on their own, and artists and labels contact successful producers with long track records of successful recordings. Most producers are hooked in to the music scene locally, regionally, and nationally and use their friends and contacts to find out what bands or artists are coming up and making a splash. Producers will often make a special trip to see an artist or band give live performances. One common thread with producers is that they simply know how to develop talent. They also know what to do in order to get talented people to give their best work. Of course there are many different kinds of talent:

Songwriter, singer, instrumentalist, performer. Usually people with marketable talent have it in two or more areas. Furthermore, star talent typically has already conquered their local or regional area, drawing people to their shows and their work. If an act cannot be successful in their own back yard, the chances of their success regionally or nationally are slim.

It is of utmost importance that the producer has the respect and trust of the artist or band they will produce, because ultimately the producer will have creative control of the recording, or at least the final say about musical choices that may cause disagreement. Disagreement is commonplace when making a recording—differences of opinion are always present. It could be as simple as a note or a chord change, all the way to the entire concept of a recording. If the artists put their trust in a producer, disagreements can be solved in a civil manner without extended bickering or even fistfights in an expensive and fragile studio! The trust between an artist and producer cannot be overemphasized. The producer has to trust that the artist will give the best performances they can give, and the artist has to trust that the producer's decisions will lead them to the promised land of recording success. Once there is trust between the two, the artist–producer relationship is ready for prime time and ready to get involved with the recording.

The next phase is to hammer out an artist–producer agreement. Such agreements spell out the producer's and the artists' duties. An artist development agreement has to do with producing the artist then shopping the artist to record labels. In return, the artist-development producer would be compensated (handsomely) if and when the artist is signed to a label deal. Some artist–producer agreements are with established artists and concentrate on producer duties and payment structures. In most cases, the contract will give the producer the final word in matters of artistic direction. For situations where a producer is brought in to work with an already known talent, the producer would not be doing an artist-development deal (the artist is already developed!) rather, a simpler contract is spelled out. Producers who are on the staff of record labels still exist, and producers in this capacity will just work under the current deal they have with their label, usually with incentives if the recording does well. Labels sometimes carry staff producers. Usually staff producers are charged with finding talent, but can also simply be assigned an act from the label.

THE INDEPENDENT PRODUCER

Through the 1950s and 1960s, record companies had house producers who had control over what songs were recorded and who recorded them. These guys were also known as "A&R men" (there wasn't much in the way of equal opportunity back then). Essentially, A&R men would find talent to be recorded and decide what songs were to be recorded, songwriters would write the songs and engineers would record the songs, with the A&R person in charge of the whole process. In the 1960s, more and more artists wrote their own songs and wanted artistic control of their own recordings. Labels began to agree to allow "outside" producers, and this was the beginning of the era of the independent producer.

Today the independent producer is often a one-person company and able to function as a complete producer—able to raise money, connect with artists, and operate in the studio (as well as engineer, thanks in no small part to digital audio workstation technology becoming so inexpensive and practical). Some independent producers have their own agents who procure jobs for them by attracting labels and artists to their great track record of work. Independent producers may also have a small staff to take care of managerial items or to even engage in other aspects of the music industry such as publishing or artist management. The idea here is to let the producer worry about producing while the staff handles managerial tasks. Another common thing is that many producers will have a production assistant. The production assistant works with the producer on projects and handles some technical items such as microphone setups and preparing songs to mix, as well as some administrative tasks that come up while in the middle of producing. In his way, the production assistant is somewhat like a second engineer and an administrative assistant.

Today's producer is typically going to want a flat producer's fee as well as a small percentage of royalties called "points" (1 point = 1%). Depending on the clout of the producer, points range from 1% to 6% of sales of the recording. Usually a producer's flat fee is considered an advance on the producer's points from the sale of the recording. Sometimes the label will demand that the producer fee be considered an advance recoupable from the artist (so now the artist has to do better than break even to start seeing money—they have to pay the producer fee as well, and this amount can be from $10,000 to $100,000 per SONG). Producer points are generally paid starting from the first sale of the recording, after any producer advance is recouped, rather than after the recording has recouped costs. This is great for the producer and can result in lots of money coming in. If a record sells 5 million copies at $10 per copy and the producer points are 5%, this works out to 2.5 million dollars! (5 million * $10 = $50 million; $50 million * 5% = $2.5 million).

TYPES OF PRODUCERS

Producers typically fall into one of the categories below. Keep in mind that in every case, a prior track record of success has paved the path to producer-dom.

Producer/Engineers are gifted in a music technology sense as well as an ability to make artistic judgments about performances and musical concepts. They start as engineers working in a studio with top producers. Usually they have a long track record of successful recordings, and have been around excellent producers long enough to learn how to handle the artistic aspects of producing. Such producers may not have a great handle on the business/contracts aspect of the music industry since they primarily deal with producing in the studio. The double threat of producer/engineers allows them to immediately translate what they want to hear into what to do in the studio to get it, without going through a separate engineer. In many cases, the producer/engineer will use an assistant engineer for the more mundane tasks like preparing the audio console for mixing and putting up microphones in the studio, so that he can concentrate more on the big picture. Many of today's producer/engineers work out of their own project studio, saving their clients studio costs and having a comfortable environment in which to work. Saving their clients money doesn't mean the producer will get nothing for the studio time in his project studio—the producer will usually still charge the record label for booking studio time at his own place.

The Artist/Producer is an artist who produces himself, or a previously (or currently) successful artist lending their experience and talent to other artists making a recording. Artist/Producers may lack the required in-studio technology skills, and might leave the engineering solely up to the engineer, while he concentrates on the overall concept of the recording. The artist/producer is usually able to relate very well to the artists while doing the recording. The recording artist in this situation might feel like he has more of an ally, especially if the artist/producer is one whom the recording artist looks up to. Also the artist/producer may or may not have a great handle on things like contracts or budgeting—these items would be left to an attorney and a business manager.

The Psychologist/Producer has a knack for motivating musicians to give their best, as well as resolving conflict. Conflicts usually arise during recordings as artistic ideas clash or as musicians perform their parts poorly. Usually, the psychologist/producer will focus in on the group's leader and get the leader on the same page, which then would trickle down to the other band members.

The Executive Producer has the wonderful ability to raise money. Such producers are also great at putting together a talented group of people required to make the recording happen. Usually the executive producer will work with a line producer who would handle the day-to-day in-studio work while they concentrate on the big picture (and raising money). The executive producer's team would include an engineer and an assistant. Executive producers excel in creating and sticking to an overall concept for a recording. Overall concept has to do with big picture items such as having a retro sound for all tracks, concentrating on aggressive musical parts, or even the concept of staying out of the way of musicians as they go through their recording process and letting the band's overall sound dictate the direction of the recording.

Co-producers share responsibilities with another complementary producer. In many cases, this could be a particular band member who assumes a leadership role while making artistic judgments during the recording. Co-producing has the advantage of using two brains to get at the final product instead of one. Many times, each producer will bring their strong point to the table—one may be a good money raiser while the other functions as a good producer/engineer. It is not uncommon for multiple producers to work on a project, especially in the rap and R&B genres. In these instances, producers often perform on the recording as well, and if the producer is well known, it can serve to introduce the new artist to the public. Co-producing can also be done as a team effort between the producer and the band, where all band members and the producer collaborate rather than giving the producer the final say-so on artistic decisions. There are cases where the band or a band friend simply wants to be credited as co-producer, even though they didn't really produce anything. This is just a matter of posturing on recording credits. Credits are a funny thing—at times they mean so much to people's resumes and can mean so little when they are fabricated.

Finally, the Complete Producer handles artistic, managerial, and technical aspects of making music recordings. Many run their own production company or artist-development company and have a long track record of music industry successes. Complete producers are rare and usually in high demand from labels and artists.

TYPES OF PRODUCTION DEALS *

1. A record label hires the producer as a full-time employee and the label's A&R head assigns projects to them. The producer would have little say in the artist to be produced but trusts that the label chose a great artist with great potential. This relationship is really the "old" way of doing things when artists had no choice about the producer to be used.

2. Independent contractor—here, the producer is an entrepreneur or has their own production company. In this situation, the labels contract with the producer, assign a budget, and expect the producer to deliver the final masters. The producer would most likely get an advance against producer royalties, right along with the artist. In this situation, both the producer and the artist invest their time and money to the project and hope to get reimbursed for their production costs as well as an advance on future royalties. They negotiate a master purchase agreement with the label. Producers might also wish to sign the talent directly, and then shop the finished product to record labels. This can be tricky because the artist or band is signed to the producer and not the label. The producer might also want pieces of the publishing from the artist even though the producer may not have written any of the songs. For unknown artists this may not be a bad thing, for it can get the artist out to the public when they otherwise would not have a shot at a label deal. Artists should, however, be careful when entering into this kind of deal with a producer—an attorney hired by the artist is usually necessary to work out the details and protect the artist from giving away too much to the producer.

3. The artist hires the producer directly, and then negotiates with the producer and the label for advances and royalties that include both the artist and producer. This relationship is pro-artist. In this way the artist is assured they get the producer they want, and the producer is more likely to acquiesce to the artist's ideas for production, since the producer is hired directly by the artist. Like most producer deals, the producer would want a flat fee plus points on the recording. The flat fee would be paid by the artist.

*(The previous section and the section on types of producers are closely derived from Baskerville's *Music Business Handbook* 7th edition.)

David Baskerville, *Music Business Handbook and Career Guide*, 7th edition (London: Sage Publications, Inc.), 332–333.

Once all contracts and financial business are agreed upon, the producer goes to work. Keep in mind that "producing" can mean a wide variety of things from sitting back and letting a band work everything out to micro-managing every musical moment by songwriting, coaching, etc. Both methods have been successful—it really comes down to personal style and the clout of the producer versus the clout of the artist. Production can be categorized into five basic steps: Pre-production, recording, editing, mixing, and post-production.

When the producer has a sure-fire hit-making machine of an artist and finalizes the general concept for the project, the producer must create a budget even if it includes some unknowns or guesses. If a label is putting up money for the project, production costs will be recoupable from the artist's earnings. If the artist takes twice the amount of time allotted to get that perfect take, it may cost more money for studio time and ultimately cost the artist even more in recoupable money. Producers involved in an artist development deal will either put up the money for the recording themselves, or they will find investors for the project.

In an artist-development production deal between the producer and artist, the main idea is to get a recording contract for the artist. If the producer is going to be involved in securing a record deal for the artist, the producer should work with the artist to prepare a full-on demo of what the artist can do, along with a business plan in order to sell the concept to a record label. Demos are no longer forgiven for being of poor quality—in order to have a record label believe in the project, the demo should be outstanding in quality and very close to what the final product would be. In order to produce the demo, the producer or artist manager may put up the necessary funds for studio fees, etc. The artist themselves may also pay for the demo recording, perhaps to show their commitment to the project.

In pre-production the producer analyzes every song the artist or band has to offer, offering suggestions or changes to make songs stronger, or in other words more "hit-ready," which will of course make the label happy. One of the things a producer (and label) will look for is the presence of a "hook," or a vocal or musical idea that is extremely memorable and catchy. We have to keep in mind that in a normal producer contract, the producer works for the label as well as the band or artist, so the producer walks a fine line between satisfying both the label and the artist. Also at this point, outside writers might be brought in to help with songwriting, or publishers might get involved in "pitching" a song to the producer and the artist to perform. Nothing is more important than picking the right songs to record. All the studio work in the world could be wasted on mediocre-quality songs, or even songs that are just not right for the artist to perform. Rehearsals are arranged for the artist or band, along with the producer to make sure that everyone knows what they intend to play on the project, not to mention practice and rehearse so that expensive studio time can be more efficiently used. A situation to avoid would be letting a band come to the studio with unfinished songs and having them work it out while expensive studio time is being billed. With everything in mind including artist comfort, costs, and quality of the studio, the producer then books time at the most appropriate studio for the project. A producer can request a "lockout," which means that the studio is booked for weeks or months at a time, and no one else can come in and use the studio. With a lockout, the band can stay set up, which makes recordings go a little faster since there is no setup after the first song is recorded. Ultimately, the artist must be comfortable in the studio, which can be a stressful environment (time is money) in order to get good performances. The artist is also very much under the microscope and any small problems with things like pitch and rhythm become glaring when put through nice studio speakers. Some studios in nice locations offer accommodations in order to attract artists. In such places, distractions from the outside world are kept to a minimum. It becomes the producer's job to minimize stress for the artist as much as possible, all in order to get the best possible performance from the artist. If the project is going to involve outside players (such as a string section or an ethnic percussion specialist), these musicians have to be hired through union contractors or hired directly and scheduled at an appropriate time. A recording engineer must be chosen, hopefully one with lots of experience with the type of music the project entails, as well as great technical know-how. Recording engineers can make or break a project, especially when they don't have vast experience with the type of music being recorded or if they are inexperienced in general. As an example, an engineer who specializes in classical music and acoustic recording may not be familiar with the techniques required to record in the R&B or urban genres, and not know how to get the electronic sounds specific to the R&B or urban scene. Another part of pre-production has to do with preparing samples and drum loops prior to entering the studio, again depending on the genre. This kind of preparation would be still part of the rehearsal and pre-production stage. It should also be noted that many producers and artists own their own project studio that can rival what they might find in the large-scale professional studios. The use of such home set-ups can greatly reduce the amount of billable studio time in the professional facility. Although certain elements (drums, for example) benefit greatly from a professionally designed room, getting that perfect vocal take in the comfort of a producer's or artist's home can be a very stress-free environment and a real money-saver. In this way, the very best vocal, and other components, can make it to the recording. As previously mentioned, stress in the studio during the next phase (recording) can be very serious. Musicians can be stressed because of time constraints while they are struggling with a part, and can start to feel the pressure. It is the producer's job to act as coach or cheerleader, or even try to lighten the mood. This kind of psychology practice is yet another thing that differentiates good producers from great ones.

Next, the project gets into the recording phase. Typically, bed tracks or basic tracks (like drums and bass) are recorded followed by overdubs. Bed tracks must be as good as they can be because these tracks are the foundation of the music. Drum recordings must sit "in the pocket" and have a very clear sense of timing throughout the entire piece, otherwise the entire recording is at risk. Even electronic drums and drum machines have to be appropriately timed for the track. Drums do not necessarily have to be recorded first, depending on the style and genre; however, most popular music recordings are done with drums first, with everyone else playing to the drums. In the case of a singer/songwriter who is used to accompanying himself, it is possible to record to a click track (a track set up to be a metronome for the entire piece) and then record everything else to the same click track. Again, everything depends on the song and the artist being recorded and getting the best performances out of them. Usually a scratch vocal is recorded along with the basic tracks so that the rest of the band can keep the vocal in mind and know where they are in the song. Sometimes the scratch vocal is so good that it becomes the "keeper" vocal. Overdubbing is a process that allows musicians to listen to previously recorded tracks and add new performances to new tracks. During this time the producer will make artistic judgments on performances and work to create the overall sound of the project. The overdub stage can take a long time to finish, especially when artists have some difficulty performing the parts or if musicians are experimenting with parts. Ultimately the artist and the producer should collaborate to get the best possible performances on the best songs with the best recorded sounds appropriate to the project. The "great rule" applies here ...

+ great songwriting
+ great performances
+ great producing
+ great engineering
+ great mixing
+ great mastering
= great song.

During recording and overdubbing, the producer's style comes to light. Some sit back and stay out of the way of the band as opposed to other producers who want to make their mark on every note being recorded. (The producer might also keep in mind that it may be a good idea to get some photos for the project's artwork while the artist is creating the music.) Producer styles cover a wide range. Since the producer is responsible for creating the overall sound of the project, a producer might be very particular as individual parts are being recorded and overdubbed since those parts all combine to create the finished product. One common practice is to record many tracks of the vocal and then pick and choose from the takes that sound the best. A vocal composite (called a "comp") is then made up from the component parts. Stories and anecdotes abound with producers and what they will go through to get at a finished product. Famed producer George Martin was known to write all of the string and ensemble arrangements for the Beatles. Another producer from the 70s would wait until all the musicians left the studio and them replace all the parts himself, overdubbing everything on his own. My favorite story involves a producer in the 70s working with a gigantic act (names withheld to protect the not-so-innocent!). The drummer of the act could simply not play in time very well, so the producer resorted to going into the room with the drummer and beating on large cardboard boxes while the drummer played so that the drummer could stay in time and on track by watching the producer. There are times when the producer must decide if the artist's band is talented enough to make the recording happen. If not, the producer has the delicate task of requiring that the band be replaced by seasoned studio veterans in order to get the tracking done in a reasonable amount of time. Studio veterans are usually expert in sight reading, which is reading music for the first time and playing perfectly as they read the chart. Also, the veteran can perform in many different styles of music. When the production phase is completed, the best performances are what remain in all the recordings.

Producers in general, and the overall sound they help to create, go out of style within about 4 to 5 years. A producer must be able to adapt to new sounds and new techniques in order to have a longer career. Certain artists may wish to produce themselves—something that some artists do more successfully than others. Artists producing themselves must be objective about the parts they are recording, which is something not always natural and easy to do. Artists producing themselves can lose perspective of the big picture and overall concept of the recording. Artists who self-produce must be able to honestly evaluate their performances, or at least rely on other band members for evaluation and ideas. On the plus side, however, is that the artist does not have to pay for a producer for the recording and if all goes well, the artist will make a recording they are proud of. Hopefully, in this case, the label will be equally proud and put the recording out! (Remember they don't have to put the recording out.)

The producer must make sure that everyone gets paid on time (the studio, the extra musicians, the engineer, etc.) and hopefully stay within the budget allowed for the record. If things go over budget, it is the producer who must go back to the label and request more money, explaining why the project is going over budget and how it will get back on track. It is not unheard of for producers to be replaced if they go over budget, even though such action will probably cost even more for the label (and ultimately the artist).

The next phase of production is editing, which is done primarily on a digital audio workstation. During editing, each track is "soloed" (played by itself) and is scrutinized. Items such as noodling in between recorded parts, various vocal noises that occur right before the vocals come in, and more, are removed. Also, if required, the engineer and producer will perform large-scale editing such as rearranging entire sections of the song in order to make the song stronger. The editing stage is also when controversial pitch correction is performed on vocal or instrumental tracks. Pitch correction changes the pitch of the vocal slightly (or a lot) so that the vocal is more in tune. Today, pitch correction is a fact of life and very few artists go without it. Pitch correction can be used subtly, for example, if a really good vocal take is recorded with lots of emotion and feeling and a few sour notes, pitch correction can be a real time saver. Otherwise the track would have to be re-recorded and you could possibly wind up with a track that is more on pitch, but with less emotion. Other uses of pitch correction are more sinister, where singers who can't stay on pitch at all are corrected into a finished, on-pitch vocal. The artist T-Pain and others have made a career out of overdoing the pitch correction until it sounds like a keyboard is playing the vocal. Vocals are not the only thing correctable in editing; drum performances are movable in time in order to make the drums more "perfect" sounding. Other elements can also be moved, for instance if the guitar player consistently plays ahead of the beat—that track can be moved in time as well.

Once everything is recorded and edited, the project enters the mix phase where a final two-track stereo master is created from all the tracks previously recorded. Sometimes an engineer who specializes in mixing is brought in. Such mixing specialist engineers can be quite expensive (upwards of

$5,000 per song). In fact, record labels frequently try to identify the one or two "singles" from the record and give those songs to the specialized mix engineer, leaving the other album cuts for a less expensive engineer to mix. A typical time frame would be to mix one song a day, with any slight corrections taking place the next day prior to the next song's mix. The time frame of one-day/one-mix can be extended for large complicated mixes with many elements. Also, artists, band mates, or the producer, might remain unhappy with the mix so more time is needed to satisfy them. In any case, the producer must ensure that the project comes together during the mix phase of production. Mixing is a process that cannot be overstated in terms of its importance since the mix of the tracks is essentially what goes out the door to the public. Special care must be taken to ensure that all elements are balanced throughout the entire song, given appropriate signal processing (or effects) and combined to create the sonic landscape the producer and artist want to hear from the song. Mixing is an art unto itself because there are so many choices to be made that are within the bounds of today's popular

music. Items to worry about are things such as the relative level of the vocal, how loud the bass drum is compared to everything else, what kind of processing the guitars should get, and on and on. If things do not come together in the mix stage, it usually means that the song either gets dropped or must be re-recorded from the beginning, correcting for whatever misguided decisions were previously made. Artists may want to be present through the entire mix process, especially if they want to be able to have some control over the direction of the mix. Other artists may elect a band member they all trust to stay with the mix engineer throughout the process. Still another situation is one where the artist will simply let the producer do the mix and make comments after the producer sends them CDs of finished mixes. However it happens, once everyone signs off on the mix, it is time for the next phase of production.

After mixing, the post-production phase of the project would begin by bringing the completed mixed project to be mastered, or prepared for manufacture. This phase is the final check before the project goes out the door for the record label to hopefully approve. (Usually by this time a representative from the label has "popped in" to check on how things are going and get a good idea of what the recording will sound like when finished.) Mastering studios have extremely accurate listening environments specializing in making final tweaks and making music play "loud" from the masters. (Professional mastering is why home recordings are nowhere near as loud off the CD as "mastered" CDs.) There has been some controversy over making CDs "loud." Without getting too technical, a CD has maximum level because of the realities of digital audio. When mastering engineers increase the average loudness with compression, it seems as if the CD is playing louder even though it has not gone over the digital maximum. (Compression is why television commercials play louder than the program show.) The controversy is that with all the compression, the audio itself does not sound as good and gives the listener ear fatigue much sooner than it should. However, making the CD "louder than the next guy's CD" is something continuously done in mastering. Lastly, the artwork for the project must be created including photos, graphic art, and lyrics. Another important part of this final process is to make sure that everyone who worked on the project is appropriately credited. To most musicians, credits are extremely important because they become part of the musician's resume. It is the producer's job to make sure that all bills are paid before delivering the final master to the record label. A producer may choose to present the final project in person in order to get label executives excited about marketing and promoting the work. If the label is excited about the project, it means that more of its resources might go toward the promotion of the recording, which is good for everyone involved. Many a great project winds up languishing and not selling well simply from a lack of promotion. The producer (and the artists' personal manager) must stay on the record label's mind in order to get favorable marketing and promotion. One has to keep in mind that a label might be taking on many projects at the same time and can properly market and promote only a few of them at once, so being the squeaky wheel who gets label attention might be a good idea.

CHAPTER 8

Touring

Touring is the fine art of taking your band out and performing in public at various venues ranging from small clubs to large arenas. How does an artist/band begin touring? When does an artist/band know when it's time to hit the road and begin a tour? These questions and many others will be answered in this chapter.

Before you even begin to think about touring with your act, you have to be a well-established, well-rehearsed, and well-known act. Now, I'm not just speaking about being known in your local city, or your local city and a couple of others close to where you live. To consider yourself ready for a possible record contract, you should be a regional success concerning performing at a variety of venues with in a four- to six-state region. What this translates into is, if you live on the east coast and you are booked at a variety of venues everywhere from New York City, New Jersey, Philadelphia, Baltimore, to Washington D.C. and you are known as the act that fills the club each and every time you perform. If you can do this, and do it consistently, chances are the record labels will come looking for you instead of you looking for them. Before I go into the specifics of touring, it needs to be explained to many local musicians that when you have a couple of weeks booked at a club, or possibly a month at two or three clubs, this is not touring ... this is gigging. There is a significant difference between being on a tour and doing gigs. I will explain the differences between the two later in this chapter. Okay, let's begin.

First, you need to take into consideration where you live. Assess how many clubs and other venues are within at least a 30- to 50-mile radius of your hometown, and this will be the geographical area in which you will strive to book gigs when you first begin to perform. The reason you have to consider such a large area to perform in is that unless you live in a large metropolitan area (and not always then), there are just not enough live-performance venues to gig. Therefore, you have to spread your wings and travel to other places to keep the money flowing in. Secondly, do not even think about performing live unless you have a minimum of four 1-hour sets of music to perform. In addition, it's not a bad idea to have at least two sets of cover songs in your repertoire. The audience will respond better to your act if you can tap into familiarity, so having known songs that are already being performed on the radio as a part of your show is not a bad idea.

Another important aspect to consider is what genre of music you will perform at these clubs. Certain geographical locations might be more into Rock music, others might be into Hip-Hop and Rap music, and others might be into Country music. Obviously, a band must find and develop its own sound and style of music. If we as musicians were to placate to anyone and everyone's personal desire of what music they would like to hear, we would be musical schizophrenics. However, this is not to diminish the statement that you should know cover tunes for the sake of familiarity to keep the listener's attention.

Now that you know when you should perform, which is when you have enough material to perform four sets, this is the time to talk about the clubs you're going to perform in. In the beginning, most of the clubs/venues will most likely be small, with a seating capacity of 100 to 150 or smaller. Don't be discouraged when only 5 to 10 people show up to the show; remember you're just beginning and the numbers will increase as your music and live show become refined. Not only are there clubs available for you to perform in, but if you live near a college town, you have your frat parties, raves, and other great college events that you can perform for as well. Many well-known acts have broken to the music industry and the live-performance scene by playing college parties.

I like the statement that author Marc Davidson uses when determining what clubs to play at. Here are some of his suggestions:

1. Pick a club that has at least a 75-person capacity. I have to say that you shouldn't be too picky. Take any gig or playing opportunity that you can when you're just beginning as a new performing act.
2. Make sure the club has a regular draw. Here's a good time to define the word "draw." Draw is the ability of the band/artist to attract people to the venue in which they're performing. The greater the draw potential an act has, the greater number of gigs you will be booked for. Draw is one of the most important items when performing at the largest venues, and is a strong determining factor with record companies as to whether or not they will sign you to a recording contract!
3. Monthly calendars. If the club that you were performing at does not put out a monthly calendar to inform their patrons as to what acts will be performing there, then do it yourself as part of your marketing campaign.
4. Clubs with sound systems and stage lighting. If the club you were performing at has its own sound system and stage lighting, chances are the sound system is tuned for that particular room and it will be a short, easy function to dial in your band instruments and vocals for that evening's performance. Moreover, it sure helps not to carry all that lousy PA equipment and lighting rigs.
5. Research. It's a wise option for the band or the band manager to research what acts have performed at the club previously. Knowing the genre of music that the act performed and the audience attendance and response is a huge indicator as to whether or not your act will be successful at that venue.
6. Stage areas. It is always a better environment for a live show if you are able to set up on a raised platform or stage. This provides better visibility for the audience to see the band, better sound reinforcement when the sound system is not blasting directly in the audience's ears, and most likely they'll have the stage entrance in which you can pull your truck, or van, or cars up to the back door stage entrance and directly load onto the stage without having to carry all of your equipment over the dance floor through the club, etc.

Now that you've discovered some of the intricacies of clubs, venues, etc., let's talk about the materials that you'll have to send them in order to acquire a gig. One of the first things you should put together for yourself either as a solo artist or for your band is what's known as a press kit, or a one sheet, or an EPK (Electronic Press Kit). For smaller venues, the kind that you are booking just to get experience and practice, a one sheet would be sufficient. The one sheet is a piece of paper that is printed only on one side, providing a comprehensive explanation and promotion of your act. Items that need to be inclusive on the one sheet would be:

- The band's name
- Various contact information: Such as the band's mailing address, e-mail address, contact phone number(s), the band's Website (if you have one ... which you should), any YouTube or MySpace sites, the band manager's name and contact information, and other pertinent information
- A recent photo of the band: Make sure the photo is something that is contemporary yet unique that will immediately draw the club owner's attention
- Make certain that the one sheet is in color. This will cost a little more money, but it is well worth it in its marketing potential

Another form of information to send to potential club owners is that of the press kit. A press kit is in essence a detailed, comprehensive portfolio of the band/artist, their music, newspaper and magazine article reviews of previous performances, a CD of their recorded material, and/or a DVD with a quick-time movie presentation of their live performance. It's very easy to get a newspaper, be it the local newspaper or even a college newspaper, to come out and see the band for half the set or a full set of music during which to write an article. Simply pick up the phone, invite a journalist to the venue that evening, and do what is commonly known as schmoozing. Schmoozing is the art practiced by all music industry professionals by which they participate in hyperbole in order to make their guest feel wanted and comfortable. I am not advocating this: Buying them a drink or two doesn't hurt either.

Let us assume now we're at the point where you as an artist or band have been performing for a minimum of two years and you have a fine live musical show. Now is the time to step up your game. One of the first things that you would want to do is have a good musical act open up for you during your shows—just not as good as your band. The audience's interpretation is that your act is of higher musical quality than the opening act. Finding an opening act is not that difficult. There are many bands in colleges and cities near you that would be happy to have the opportunity to perform live with an established band for a nominal fee. The fee is negotiable depending on the opening act's musical prowess and most importantly their draw potential, as their fans might become your fans and increase your fan base. Lastly, some of the basic administrative/accounting work needs to be done prior to performing the gig. You want to begin to focus on promoting the show, which could mean advertising it on your band's Website, sending out flyers, putting an ad in the local newspaper, or simply by word of mouth. Step out, call the local radio stations, and try to get the show mentioned on the air.

Correspond with the club owner updating them on the progress you've made promoting the show; find out what they have done in promoting your show. Lastly, invite people who can enhance your career such as radio disc jockeys, local newspaper journalists, and talent agents to your show. Of course, you know that you will have to give them free passes to the show, and maybe other items such

as a free CD. As it's been said before, you've got to spend money to make money.

We are going to jump ahead assuming that your band has done everything previously mentioned and you are a very successful regional act. So much so, that now you are being approached by some Independent and Major record labels that are in the process of shopping a deal.

IMPORTANT NOTE: When you are at the point in your career in which record labels are shopping a deal with you, never represent yourself/ your band! The individuals who work in the record industry are very clever; they know all the tricks in the book to persuade young musicians to sign contractual agreements that are generally not to their benefit as far as longevity in a musical career is concerned. When you are at this point of your career, make certain that your artist manager has the wherewithal to contact a reputable, experienced entertainment attorney who has recently negotiated new record contracts. If you don't know any entertainment attorneys, you can always contact the managers of artists who are signed and ask who represents them, you can contact a record company and ask the same question, or keep up with all of the news in the industry. Obviously, you don't want to go into an attorney's office that has 24-karat gold-plated doorknobs, nor do you want to do business with an entertainment attorney who drives up in 1982 Chevy Monte Carlo that desperately needs a paint job and an internal cleaning to get rid of the musty smell of it sitting in the bottom of a lake for two months. I think you understand where I'm going with this.

SUCCESS! You have acquired a record deal, you have gone through the process of recording your new album, and the record label has mass-produced and distributed free goods to some influential radio stations across the country where your music has been well received. Congratulations! Now it's time to go out and prove to the world you are worthy to compete with the other major artists who are in the top 20 on the Billboard charts.

As a side note please remember this, when you are pursuing the elusive record deal, do so not with the mindset that the local band in your small burg is your competition, nor is the pseudo-regional successful band your competition. Your competition is those artists who are in the top 20 on the Billboard charts. Those are the artists you must strive to compete with if you want to have any chance of being signed to a record deal.

Let's put together our American tour team. Note: Most personal managers do not go out on tour with their artist/act for the entire tour. They will, however, be present for special shows or during different times of the tour to make certain everything is operating smoothly. The times that they are not there they will be negotiating the next record deal or the next tour, or anything else that involves the growth and success of their artist's/band's career.

The touring team and their roles

1. Managers. There are several different types of managers who will accompany the artist/band on the road. Road Manager. This person is directly responsible for everything that happens with the act/artist while on tour. They will coordinate everything from the tour itinerary, hotel accommodations, communication with the concert promoter concerning items of ticket

sales, merchandising setup, concert security, insurance, sale of artist/band merchandise with merchandisers at the show; they will make certain that all parameters within the concert contract are being honored, have open communications with the record label representative, and most of all tend to every need of the artist/band, including where to be and when to be at a specific place during the day, and generally meet all of the needs and obligations of the band/artist. The road manager must play the role of friend, band psychologist, police officer, medical doctor, and any other need that the band may have. The road manager must address and have some type of answer for everything to make certain the show occurs without a hitch and on time. This is an extremely time-consuming and difficult job, and there are individuals in the music industry who have trained and have acted as road managers for other bands/artists. Find them, interview them, and choose the best for your band/artist.

2. Stage Manager. The stage manager is directly responsible for all activities that occur on the stage involving stage crew, lighting crew, union members at various large performance halls, sound crew, and basically everything that involves putting on the live show for the audience that day. Most stage managers also have years of experience with other bands. Some have been on-stage monitor, or main house sound engineers. Alternatively, they may have been a personal road crewmember for a specific player or singer in a band or bands they have worked with previously. The stage manager is in direct contact with the road manager, and both might be in contact with the personal manager. The stage manager would be in charge of two other important positions: The sound man or sound people and the road crew. The road crew is commonly referred to as the roadies or the band technicians. Let's start with the sound people. Bands, musicians, artists, please hear me out on this one. Treat the sound people as a member of the band, because in essence they are! I love the one Gary Larson cartoon where it is the last day of the sound person's job, and the band is behind chicken wire while the audience is throwing bottles, food, tables, and anything else they can hurl at the band. Why … because the soundman is turning up the Suck Knob on the mixing console. After you've been on the road for a number of years you'll find this quite hilarious and at the same time quite frightening. No matter how incredible the performance is that you are putting on stage, if it sounds bad in the mains (the speakers that face the audience), then it's just not going to be received as a good show. Professional sound people can command thousands of dollars per week in wages, including per diem. Of course, this is dependent upon their background and who they've toured with. Secondly, but as important is the job of the stage monitor's sound person. I would go so far to say that this might even be more important than the mains, because if the band is dissatisfied with what they hear on the stage it will directly affect their performance. And, the monetary compensation that this person can earn is the same as that of the main sound person based on experience and bands they have toured with.

3. Accountant. This person will deal directly with the concert promoter in tandem with the road manager in the collection of monies earned for ticket sales and merchandising. The accountant of the band generally has a degree in accounting—the plethora of details that go into putting on a live concert can be overwhelming and you need someone who has the experience to account for every penny. The accountant must deal with keeping all the books and records, spreadsheets, bank accounts and petty cash, all expenses, payroll, and then develop reports for the personal manager and possibly the record company. You are not dealing with

hundreds of dollars here, but hundreds of thousands to possibly one or two million per show, depending on the draw of the band/artist.

4.   Concert Promoter. The concert promoter can be a single individual or a set of individuals who own or rent a concert venue to bands/artists that book shows in their city. The concert promoter will generally deal directly with the personal manager and the road manager. A good personal manager will negotiate a contract with the concert promoter in which 50% of the guarantee that is a flat rate paid to the band, to be paid prior to the band's arrival at the concert promoter's venue. The remainder of monies owed by the concert promoter to the band can be determined either on a flat rate, ticket sales, or a combination of both. The concert promoter is directly responsible for the safety of both the artist/band and the audience who comes to see the performance. Therefore, it is of vital importance that not only the concert promoter but also the band's/artist's manager will carry insurance for protection from unforeseen accidents that may occur during touring. The concert promoter will establish what is known as a hall fee, a fee negotiated based on the draw of the band, the size of the venue, the number of security members to be hired, emergency medical technicians, transportation for the artists/bands to and from the venue, backstage accommodations such as dressing rooms, area to eat lunch and/or dinner, and more. The concert promoters will generally negotiate a percentage of ticket sales for their participation in the band's/artist's performance. One of the most important things that the concert promoter must address is that of the concert Rider.

5.   The concert rider is one of the most detailed and important aspects of the concert contract negotiations. The rider is the all-inclusive explanation of all equipment needed for the performance, all ancillary equipment needed backstage, the specifics of food and drink in the artist's/band's dressing rooms, sound, lighting, exact positioning of all staging, lighting, and musical equipment, and much more. We've all heard stories and have actually seen certain concert riders of particular artists that seemed, and actually were, outrageous. For example, artists or bands requiring a large number of live plants for their dressing rooms, a huge array of alcoholic beverages, special lighting for backstage ... to get into the mood, specific dietary needs and when I say specific, I really mean specific. Then, there are those acts that require what we would construe as strange requests. Such as four boxes of Magnum condoms, an assortment of pornographic magazines, no brown M&Ms in the candy bowl, accommodations for the artist's/band's pets, accommodations for their significant others, and the list goes on. Now the rider is an important aspect in ensuring the concert runs smoothly. Items requested such as specific musical equipment, microphones, staging for safety purposes, stage or in-ear monitors, and more are the definite aspects that are important to include in a concert rider. For those of you who are interested in finding out more about this, and actually seeing some of the extremely strange requests of certain artists, simply Google Concert Rider and then the artist's name that you're interested in. Enjoy.

6.   Tour Itinerary. The tour itinerary is the Bible of the road, an all-inclusive, detailed accounting of everything that will occur during the band's/artist's tour. The tour itinerary will include hotels where the band and road crew are staying, transportation, times for sound checks, set up and tear down, restaurants and entertainment places located near the hotel where you're staying, radio and other types of interviews, green room activities backstage, show time, concert promoter information, concert venue information, all addresses and phone numbers needed, and things that you would think would be normal and a band member would know,

but we don't, such as departure times of the tour bus or plane, special band meetings, when to eat, when to prepare for the show in relation to getting dressed, warming up on your instrument or vocals, and every other tiny detail that would be important for that concert day's activities. I can attest to the fact that if it were not for tour itineraries, my whole band and I would be lost. So, future personal managers and road managers, study up on how to write a comprehensive yet understandable tour itinerary.

What are some other items that we need to consider concerning going on the road and touring? If you are the personal manager or the road manager, you will want to keep a journal of all activities that occurred on tour. The first purpose of this journal is to create a database of contacts within the music industry; include any pertinent information relating to the venue in which you performed, local unions such as the AFM (American Federation of Musicians), local talent agents, and special guests who may have attended the show who could have future positive consequences on the band's music future.

The business of concert promotion is not just that of large-venue performances. It has been said that concert promoters are the buyers of entertainment. We could break down this category into three main categories. First, the large venues and performance arenas. Second, there are midscale arts events that would include symphonic, chamber music, opera, dance, and musical theater events. Third, there is that of the local venue concerts, which we have discussed in the form of clubs, small venues, private parties, etc.

What are the legal entities that personal managers and sometimes bands/artists must do business with? One, which we have discussed, is the local musicians union, or the AFM. Many cities state that they require you to be a member of the local union or you may not perform at many venues. This is not the case. I have found that in most to all cities, bands can and do perform at most venues without being members of the local union. However, if you reside in Los Angeles, Las Vegas, Nashville, New York City, and a few other choice cities, it is required that you are a member of the union. So, if you live in one of these areas, look up your local union, give them a call, and join up.

Many books discuss specific fee arrangements on how the concert promoter will pay the artist or band. One is called the flat fee, or what is known as a basic guarantee. The individuals involved agree on a fee to be paid to the act regardless of how much income the promoter brings in. The second would be the flat fee plus percentage. This is an arrangement wherein again a flat fee is agreed upon, plus an additional percentage of ticket sales is paid to the band/artist. Third is percentage of ticket sales. Many of the bands out there playing local clubs, and you may be one of them, are very familiar with this concept as it entails agreeing upon a percentage of what is taken in at the door, or ticket sales. Last, there is the percentage versus a flat fee. Through contractual negotiations, the band will take either a percentage of some ticket sales, or a flat fee, whichever is greater.

Other agencies/unions you may have to deal with during touring include the American Guild of Variety Artists, which deals with venues such as casinos and fairgrounds. The Screen Actors Guild will represent artists who perform in movies. The American Federation of Television, Radio and Recording handles performers who sing on television. One interesting side note about this organization is that even if you lip sync—which means pretend to perform a song while a sound recording is being performed in the background—if you open your mouth, you will earn royalties. Nice. Other organizations that deal with arts administration: The Association of Performing Arts Presenters, which deals with orchestras, opera, and like musical genres; and the National Endowment for the Arts, which is likely the largest source of funds for the nonprofit arts sector in the United States. The caveat to being involved with arts administration performances is that the majority are funded through federal grants or private donations.

Touring is a necessity for artists in today's music industry! In the not-too-distant past, touring served the purpose of promoting the sale of a band's or artist's new recording. Due to the creation of new digital technologies, the Internet provides us with most of the marketing parameters needed in order to convince the buyer to purchase the artist's/band's material. Touring has now become a function of earnings for the artist/band instead of the sale of their CDs and remuneration via mechanical and other types of royalties. This is particularly true for the Hip-Hop and Rap genres.

Regardless of what genre of music you perform, touring is an extremely important and integral part of your musical career.

CHAPTER 9

Music Publishing

After writing a song, the songwriter retains ownership of the song and there are certain rights that come with ownership. These are the right to mechanical royalties, the right to make the first recording, the right of public performance, print rights, synchronization rights, grand rights, and rights to new media versions. Before we get into publishing, let's first sort out the various rights.

Mechanical Royalties are money paid to songwriters and music publishers from the sale of recordings containing a copyrighted and owned song. (Interestingly, the term "mechanical" comes from the days when player pianos were popular. They used a mechanical piano roll, which functioned somewhat like a complex music box. As the roll moved over the playback mechanism, the piano would play itself.) The right of first recording means the songwriter has the right to make the first recording of the song before anyone else can touch it. After the first recording, anyone can record the song as long as they pay the appropriate compulsory license. Compulsory means that the copyright owners are compelled to let others record the song for a fixed mechanical rate. By law, the current standard mechanical royalty rate at the time of this writing is 9.1 cents for a recording of a song that lasts five minutes or less, with 1.75 cents per additional minute for songs over five minutes long. Digital downloads of songs use the same rate of 9.1 cents. All of this means that for every recording of the song sold, the songwriter and publisher would get 9.1 cents. Controlled composition means that the artist/writer owns the copyright for the song and therefore "controls" the song. Record labels came up with the idea of controlled composition clauses in their contracts, which is a way of reducing the amount they have to pay for mechanical royalties. This kind of clause will allow the record company to pay 75% of the statutory rate, or 6.825 cents per song. Furthermore the label imposes a maximum of ten times the reduced rate, even if there are more than ten songs on the recording. Controlled composition clauses are almost standard for recording contracts.

Performance rights are income derived from radio and television play as well as from works performed in shows. This is where PROs (performing rights organizations) come into play for the publisher and writer. In the U.S., the three PROs are ASCAP, BMI, and SESAC. Writers and publishers sign up exclusively with one of the three PROs in order to register their works. The primary purpose of the PRO is to pay writers and publishers wherever there is a public performance of their copyrighted music. This would include playing the song over the radio in a store, live concert performances of the song, and everything in between. PROs collect money a variety of ways. They levy fees on all performance venues—basically everywhere music is played is subject to some fee from the PRO, and the blanket fee would give the location permission to play any of the songs in the catalog of the PRO. Additionally, the PROs charge radio stations a percentage of their gross earnings, allowing them to play songs from their respective catalogs. Lastly, PROs generate income by charging a fee to all network and cable stations, requiring them to issue a log of every song played in any broadcast. After all the money is collected, the PRO deducts their business expenses and administration fees, and the remaining funds are distributed to writers and publishers according to how often their copyrighted music was played. All three PROs use a complex formula to estimate how many performances oc-curred, since there would be no way of logging each and every time a particular song is played in the thousands of venues across the country. Performances logged from radio and television are weighted in different ways according to factors such as time of day and size of the broadcast market, and other factors such as position on the "charts" (Billboard, etc.). Other factors for television include how the song was used (background, title track, etc.). In the end, money gets distributed to both publisher and writer members according to how many performances were calculated. Writers and publishers are paid directly regardless of their contractual relationship with record labels or each other. Typically, every dollar of performance royalty income is split 50-50 between the writer and the publisher of the work. Writers with their own publishing company get both halves, or 100% of the money gener-ated. Most industrialized countries have their own PRO along with reciprocal agreements with the organizations in the U.S. so that a song from either country's roster of artists will generate income for the appropriate writer and publisher in their home country. Each of the PROs offers their own brand of benefits, namely in the form of conferences and workshops, especially if you reside in one of the main recording centers of the U.S. (New York, Nashville, and Los Angeles). It is a good idea, if possible, to get to know some of the representatives of your particular PRO since many of the reps are in contact with movers and shakers in the recording industry as well as the film and TV world—they may be able to open doors for talented, unknown writers.

Printing rights have to do with the sale of printed music. During the early twentieth century, print music publishing was the primary source of income for publishers and writers. Piano was the most popular instrument and most people would learn music from a piano score. Demand for piano music decreased after radio and phonorecords became popular (thanks to rock and roll!) since more and more musicians started learning music by ear rather than from the printed page. Today, print music publication is a less substantial part of the music industry pie but still represents a good piece. Royalty rates are 8 to 12 cents on a piece of sheet music that would sell for 3.95. Print music in many cases requires that the song get rearranged to be played solely on piano, or made easier to play. Although arrangements are able to be copyrighted, most of this work is done under a work-for-hire basis and does not generate royalties for the arranger. Today's print music publishers are larger companies that have bought up smaller publishers or that have the catalog of a large full-service publisher. Hal Leonard and Alfred Music are the two largest, specializing in all aspects of print music publication from popular to educational. Mel Bay is another print publishing company that specializes in instruc-tional music for guitar as well as other instruments. Educational print music publishing is a large part of the printed music industry specializing in school ensembles like choral and band music. Since print music is easily made available on the Web, publishers must work to protect their copyrights. The National Music Publishers Association attempts to shut down as many copyright violators as possible. A large part of the print publishing picture has to do with instructional music for students, including kindergarten through high school (K–12) all the way up to university students. Instructional music

for all the instrument groups (strings, winds, brass, and percussion) as well as the most popular (piano and guitar) is mainly found in retailers who sell and rent such instruments to students. Serious (classical) music publishers make their money by selling the classics (in most cases public domain music). They also have the function of publishing newly composed work, even though there is not much income generated from this kind of copyrighted music. In most cases, serious music publishers rent out the various parts of the piece (all the separate parts of an orchestra have their own specific parts, for example). In order to sell this kind of music, most publishers will engage in a direct-mail campaign to educators, schools, and universities, or create advertisements in popular music education trade magazines such as Music Educator's Journal. The process of creating printed music requires music arrangers (to arrange the recorded music for specific instruments), music editors, and people who specialize in creating print-ready documents for the actual printing press.

Synchronization rights govern the use of music in synchronization to picture—in other words, music in film. Generally there is no set rate for licensing music for this purpose, so each license is negotiated separately between the film or TV producer and the publishing company. Factors such as the importance of the song in the particular scene, whether the song was used in the end credits or title sequence, all determine the amount of money to charge for the license. A general figure would be $15,000 to $30,000 per use, but this number can go well over $30,000 depending on the song's popularity. Very popular songs command such high fees when they are featured prominently in the movie or TV show. Medium- to large-budget films and TV shows make use of a music supervisor who finds and contracts for music to be used, in consultation with the show's director and producer. If the television show goes into syndication, or if the film is shown regularly on television (especially prime time), a substantial amount of money could come in from the PRO. Sometimes the promise of performance-oriented royalties is enough for the publisher to reduce the negotiated publisher fee, with the thinking that placement on the show or film could mean a boost to an artist's/writer's career. If an original recording were to be used on a film or television show, the show's producer would have to contract with the publishing company for use of the song and the record label for use of the sound recording. Such fees are completely negotiable and there are no standard rates. Most music written for commercials is done on a work-for-hire basis; therefore, the writer simply would get an agreed-upon fee for writing the music, and no other royalties. If an existing song is to be used, the same holds true as it does for movies and television shows—the fee is negotiated. Such negotiations take into consideration the size of the target audience, financial strength of the company, etc. There is also the matter of exclusivity—the commercial product owner would not want the same song to be used for other products or a competing product, and such exclusivity warrants an increased fee for the publisher and writer.

Grand rights generate royalties from the use of music in plays and musical theater. Typically the writer (of the play), the lyricist, and the composer share in a 6% royalty rate on the gross receipts from the box office. For new plays and musical theater productions, a producer will "option" the work for one to three years while raising money to bring the play to life. The option involves the producer paying the writer, lyricist, and composer as an advance to be deducted when the play is finally performed (that is ... if the play is performed). Grand rights can earn substantial amounts of money if the play becomes a Broadway smash hit. There will be income from the initial run of the play sometimes lasting for years. Furthermore, there will be income from touring groups putting on the play, from a soundtrack recording, and from smaller local and regional groups putting on the play. Songs that are already composed require a negotiated fee with the publisher, who will usually negotiate fees similar to other music being used in the production.

Rights to "new uses" of music involve ringtones, ringback tones, and new media such as video games. The current statutory rate for ringtones and ringbacks is 24 cents. This area of use involves ever-changing types of media and uses of music, all of which still must be licensed though a publisher. The Guitar Hero and Rock Band franchises have been a boon to publishers, and record labels if original recordings are used. Many video games for the big three—Xbox, PlayStation, and Wii—use prominently featured music from the pop world and have the budgets to pay big money for their use. These rights also include things like greeting cards and toys that play music.

Music publishing has to do with assigning and exploiting all of these rights in order to make money. Music publishing has come a very long way from simply publishing printed music. In fact, it has transformed into an integral part of modern music business. While printed music is certainly still a substantial part of music publishing, most of the world of publishing has to do with copyright (as in who owns what) and exploiting copyrighted music (trying to make money from copyrighted music). Most money comes from public performances of copyrighted works through the performance rights organizations ASCAP, BMI, and SESAC; and mechanical royalties of copyrighted works, which would come from record labels. Publishers vary in size and scope from the giants (Warner/Chappell, EMI, BMG, MCA, etc.) to companies with one employee barely doing anything—except for hopefully collecting money! Music publishing is one of the primary sources of income for artists, especially those who write and record their own songs.

The heart of a publishing agreement or contract (also known as a publishing "deal") works by assigning to the publisher ownership of a copyrighted song or songs. In return for the copyright, the publisher agrees to go after income for the publisher (of course), as well as the songwriter. This is usually advantageous to both parties because the writer can concentrate on writing good songs, and the publisher can concentrate on administering the business aspects of publishing for the writer. Traditionally, this is a 50/50 arrangement—for every $1.00 of income, the songwriter would get 50 cents and the publisher would get 50 cents. The songwriter's fifty percent of the income goes in his or her pocket, and the publisher uses its fifty percent to pay for business expenses, and (hopefully) profit.

A publisher's first task is to collect good songs and sign good songwriters to a publishing deal. This can be easier said than done. While there are many songwriters out there, truly talented writers are scarce, especially writers with the ability to write songs for other artists. A next task is to record demos of the writer's songs. This can be done in an in-house studio that the publisher operates or at a commercial facility, or even at the writer's home if they have a project studio. This demo is one of the most important sellers of the music—the better the demo quality, the better the chances of getting another artist to perform the song on their record. In fact in this writer's opinion, there are no such things as demos any more. Previously demos were less-than-great quality recordings used just to get the idea of the song across. With today's technology, demos should be just about to the quality of a finished professional recording or people do not have patience to listen. Next, the publisher has to find a way to get artists or producers to use the publisher's songs on an album or single that will hopefully be a runaway success with lots of airplay and records sold. This is where relationships between the publisher and artists, personal managers, and producers really come into play since all three are always looking for songs to record and perform. A publisher would be in constant contact with music supervisors to place songs in films, television, and advertising campaigns and then proceed to negotiate fees for their use. Airplay of a copyrighted work counts as a public performance—and this is where ASCAP, BMI, or SESAC kicks in, paying out money based on a calculation of the number of performances over a given amount of time. Publishers also generate income from mechanical royalties of recordings. For each of the publisher's songs on a recording, there is a mechanical royalty paid to the publisher and the songwriter. Lastly, there is still money to be made selling printed sheet music, mostly in the field of education (Wind Ensembles, Marching Bands, Choir, etc.) and piano/vocal scores. Sometimes including the printed music in a folio of all one artist or various artists can be lucrative depending on the royalty rate for such inclusion. A "Most Favored Nation" clause exists in some print music agreements where if there is one hit song commanding a particular royalty, then all the rest of the songs in the folio get the same royalty.

Other important jobs a publisher does is to try to develop talent on their own talent roster by offering critiques and guidance as to what end users are looking for, in order to help the writers write songs that can make it on someone else's recording. Furthermore, the publisher might actively find song collaborators for their writers to help their creative juices flow and to put two or more creative heads together in order to make strong songs. Collaborations can lead to some issues regarding how much each collaborator contributed to the particular song. Typically for two collaborators the split would be 50-50. Sometimes, if perhaps one songwriter wrote the verses and choruses and another wrote the bridge only, the 50-50 relationship might be adjusted to 65-35 or some other arrangement, hopefully without hurt feelings. Things like this should be hammered out ahead of time so that everyone stays happy throughout the songwriting process. If a songwriter is also an artist, the publisher might work hard to get the writer a recording contract, therefore guaranteeing that the songs will make it onto an album and possibly generate income. The publisher may even own a record label for just this purpose. Administratively, the publisher should make sure all songs on their catalog are properly registered with the copyright office as well as the performing rights organizations (ASCAP, BMI, SESAC) just to be sure that all copyrights are protected and ready to receive income when some is generated. Occasionally the publisher will ask for audits of the various money organizations to make sure all unpaid money gets paid. There are times when large corporations can drag their feet in paying out what they owe! The publisher should take care in developing and exploiting all industry contacts in film, television, advertising, and record companies, making sure they are up to date on all the publisher's latest song collections.

ARTIST/WRITER-OWNED COMPANIES

These are small individually owned publishing companies that are set up for writers who don't have a publishing deal, or for writers who simply want to keep more of the money that comes from income sources. In an artist-writer-owned company, the writer gets the normal 50% writer's share AND the 50% publisher's share, or in other words, 100% of the money. However, unless the writer is a superstar with lots of other artists waiting in line to record their songs (like songwriter Diane Warren), such companies do not necessarily have the national and international market presence and ability to promote songs to those who might use the songs, such as music producers, film producers, and other artists. In most cases, artist- and writer-owned publishing companies will have only that particular artist's or writer's catalog of songs to deal with. Such companies can be set up rather inexpensively (sometimes for under $400) and if you are any kind of writer, it might be a good idea to set up your own publishing company just in case a publisher comes along who wants to sign you—in that situation there might be a chance to get a co-publishing deal or an administration-only deal (more on those later).

FULL-LINE PUBLISHERS

In contrast to individually owned companies are giant publishing companies with large catalogs of songs they control. Such music publishers have entire departments of people dedicated to specific tasks that the publisher performs. In most cases, these companies are part of some even larger record or film company—a good example would be Warner/Chappell, which reigns over a million song copyrights. Such companies will have an upper administration handle business affairs and an accounting department to handle income from royalties and licenses, cash flow, and payments to employees and writers. Licensing and copyright departments are there to navigate the complex area of copyright law as it pertains to the company's copyrights, determining ownership of copyrights, and deal with the Harry Fox Agency on mechanical royalties and licensing fees. A legal department (with staff attorneys) would handle contracts and contract negotiations with writers and sub-publishers The job of acquiring new material is one of the most important areas of publishing since garnering new copyrights and exploiting them represents new (and more) income for the publisher. Promotion departments try to get their company's songs into the hearts and minds of producers and artists, as well as movie producers and advertising firms. Full-line publishers will usually have an international presence as well, with company divisions that cover music copyrights in most foreign territories, or as a co-publisher (more on that later). Another way full-line publishers acquire new material is to buy out independent publishers and take over their entire catalog of copyrighted music; the thinking is that the full-line company can better exploit the catalog than the smaller company.

INDEPENDENT PUBLISHERS

Independent publishers are simply publishers that are not connected to one of the full-line publishers. Although these publishers do the same kinds of things that all publishers do (deal with copyrights, song placement, etc.), they are smaller, often more nimble, and better able to exploit and place songs quicker than their larger counterparts. There are a number of independent publishers that simply perform the function of copyright administration—accounting, licensing, collecting royalties, taking calls and requests to use songs, and legal services—all for a piece of the publisher's gross royalty for the monies they collect, usually in the area of 10% to 15%. This kind of arrangement is known as an administration-only deal.

SUB-PUBLISHERS

In most cases, publishing companies use firms that specialize in printing music in order to realize income from printed music. A typical situation would be one where the printing company licenses copyrighted music from the publisher, creates printed editions, and gives the publisher a smaller cut of the proceeds, because the printer has to pay for all the pre-printing and printing costs. Instances where the printed version features a picture of the artist who recorded the piece of music (not necessarily the music composer) may provide some kind of royalty to that artist in return for using their likeness to sell the music. Another example of a sub-publisher would be a foreign sub-publisher working in a foreign market that is hired to perform publisher duties in that territory for a cut of the publishing income. This can be done through one of the full-line companies that have subsidiary companies in the foreign market, or by dealing directly with an independent publisher in that market. It is important to know that income from public performances from foreign sources goes directly from that country's PRO directly to the writer, while the publisher in that country gets the publisher's share, and then has to pay the American publisher according to whatever deal they worked out. For example, if an American publishing company had a 75/25 deal with a publishing company in Japan for public performance income, 50% of the money goes directly from the Japanese PRO (performing rights organizations) directly to the American PRO, which forwards it to the writer. The other 50% is divided up so that the Japanese company gets 25% of the publisher's 50% and the American company gets 75% of the publisher's 50%. In other words, for every $1.00 of income from Japanese public performance, 50 cents goes to the writer, 37.5 cents goes to the American company (75% of .50), and 12.5 cents goes to the Japanese company. Mechanical royalties and synchronization licenses work in similar fashion, depending on the deal made between the publisher and the sub-publisher. Another area of foreign sub-publishers is to provide English translation for recordings and re-record the vocal parts in the native language. The foreign publisher engages in similar activities as the American publisher—trying to exploit copyright in the foreign country, getting foreign artists to perform songs, pushing for placement in television and advertisement, and collecting foreign royalties from that country's PRO. These agreements are typically for one-year terms with a renewable option by the American publisher. Such deals can be made for single songs, a particular artist, or the entire publisher's catalog, usually with advances paid by the foreign publishing company, again, all depending on who has the most bargaining power.

CO-PUBLISHING

There are many instances where two or more writers, each with different publishing companies, collaborate on a particular song. This kind of thing necessitates a co-publishing arrangement. Essentially, publishing income gets split between the two (or more) companies and the writers. In the case of two writers, a normal agreement would be a 50-50 split where each company and writer gets 50% of what they normally would get. In other words, the publishers each get 50% of their 50% publishing share, and the writers get 50% of the writers' share, or in another way of putting it everyone gets 25% of the total publishing income. Things get more complex in terms of percentages where there is more than one writer or if one writer writes more of the song than another; however, ASCAP, BMI, and SESAC will honor the various percentages of the writers. Administration of synchronization rights can get somewhat complex and has to be worked out in terms of which publisher administers synchronization rights, otherwise it may get muddled as to who controls the composition when negotiating and collecting monies. You can't have more than one publisher licensing synchronization rights because the other publisher(s) might be bound to that agreement, and may not agree with the use. Most times it is best to work out which publisher will administer synchronization.

Another example of co-publishing occurs when a recording artist owns his or her own publishing, and the record label publishing affiliate wants in on the publishing as well. Usually this agreement is also set at the 50% mark. In this case, the writer would get the normal writer's share (50%) plus 50% of the publisher's share—which would be 75% of the total publishing income—and the label's publishing company would get 25% of the publishing income.

SONG PLUGGERS

Mostly based in Nashville, song pluggers are people connected to the publishing industry and the music industry who have access to major movers and shakers—artists, producers, publishers, and record labels. For a monthly fee they promise to give a certain number of song pitches per month of their client's catalog, and then report back each month on the pitches they made and any feedback. Varying levels of writers will make use of song pluggers—some with publishing deals and some looking for publishing deals ... all trying to get their songs in front of music-industry decision makers. Song pluggers run from about $400 per month to as high as $1,500 a month.

HARRY FOX AGENCY

The National Music Publishers Association (NMPA) created the Harry Fox Agency as a service to provide mechanical-licensing guidelines and to issue various kinds of licenses, usually for a service fee of 6.5% of mechanical royalty income. With over 28,000 publishers worldwide, the HFA is able to issue the largest number of licenses for the use of music in both the physical and digital formats. Harry Fox Agency does not issue licenses for public performances (ASCAP, BMI, and SESAC do that), but does issue mechanical licenses for works imported into the U.S. from foreign music publishers. The HFA is actually quite a high-tech entity, making use of their Songfile® software tool for short-run mechanical licensing.

In an exclusive publishing deal, the publisher will offer a weekly "draw" or salary in exchange for owning publishing rights to any songs the writer would write; the amount of draw factors in the writer's track record. Sometimes the publishing company will fund demo recordings keeping records of costs and holding them against the writer's future royalties. Usually there are specific delivery requirements, such as the writer may have to deliver ten commercially acceptable songs within one year; failure to do so would end the agreement.

SONGWRITING AND TRYING FOR A PUBLISHING DEAL

First of all, songwriting is not for the weak-hearted. Songwriting is a tough business and full of the answer "no." How does one get "yes" for an answer? Everything starts with your songs. Your songs have to be of excellent quality, period. Everything about your song has to be great, starting with a great melody that is recognizable, yet still new and different enough to be interesting. If you are a student of songwriting, you will know that hit song melodies have a balance between stepwise motion and interval jumps or angular motion. Hit song melodies are always memorable. The chord structures of a hit song are usually a simultaneous combination of standard (like many songs before) and with a new twist (unlike most songs before). The interesting thing about chord structure is that there really is nothing new to be done, only in how your chords are presented, the timing between chords, and so on.

Of course, melody fits right in to the chord structure as well. One way of achieving a great melody is to come up with many different melodies over the same chord progressions and pick which one is the strongest. Most songwriters will constantly tinker with melody until the demo is finished. Songs should get to the "point" within thirty to forty seconds, which means, they get to the memorable chorus by that time. Most hit songs contain a bridge or departure from the verses and choruses that somehow magically leads right back in to the chorus or another verse using chord structures, melody, or both. (My favorite bridge ever is on the Eagles song "New Kid in Town," which contains a brilliant modulation, or key change). Once you think you have a sure-fire hit, the thing to do is play your song for as many people as possible and ask questions such as "what did you like about it?" and "did you lose interest in the song at any point?" Keep in mind that your mom and dad will love everything you do, so while they are great for your ego, they don't really do you much good with your song. It is best to find people with honest opinions, such as other musicians you admire (and can get access to) and simple everyday people who love to listen to music. These kinds of folks will give you the best feedback. Once you've gathered as much feedback as possible, it will be necessary to go back and make changes and adjustments to your song, further refining it into a well-oiled, no-problems-whatsoever kind of hit song. I always suggest to songwriters to go for "compact" writing without too much repetition, yet with enough repetition to drive home the main point of the song. I could go on and on about songwriting, so I will. Introductions should be brief and there should only be one introduction. I've had many students write introductions that were longer than the verses and choruses! Remember the longer the introduction, the shorter the time you should take to get to the chorus. There are a number of songs that even start with the chorus—I bet you can think of some examples. Reaching back from my decade, two examples would be "You Give Love a Bad Name" from Bon Jovi, and "Walk on Water" by Eddie Money.

Lyrics are just as important as anything else in a song; some writers excel and some struggle. Entire books have been written on lyric writing (as well as songwriting). Good lyrics are poetic, familiar, new, not contrite, and compacted as much as possible. Lyrics are poetic in that many follow a syllabic and a rhyming scheme. Familiar in terms of subject of the lyrics—people should know about the feeling or emotion they convey. New in that there should be some kind of fresh take. There are so many love songs already recorded, yet songwriters still find ways of making lyrics about love new. There are many examples of a syllabic or a rhyming scheme involved with lyrics. On the other hand there are some that do not rhyme, which brings me to my next point. For every rule of songwriting there are always exceptions, usually more than a few. There are lots of "rules" to songwriting to be followed or to be broken, all depending on what might be best for the song at hand.

Now that we have digressed enough for a quick rundown of Songwriting 101, let's go into some other areas. One of the best things you can do is to affiliate with one of the Performing Rights Organizations. BMI and SESAC have no fee, ASCAP has a fee and expects you to have already published something or have a distributed recording. All three have something to offer, namely songwriting workshops. You should be attending those regularly whenever you can. NSAI (National Songwriters Association International) is another organization that holds songwriting workshops. These are great places to get the professional feedback we talked about earlier in this section.

OK, now that you have attended the workshops, and have written and rewritten your song a few times, and you are sure to have a hit song, here is the difficult part. Write another one. In fact, write 10 to 20 more. A publisher is going to want to see that they have a prolific songwriter on their hands before extending a deal. This is very important because it will also let you pick and choose which songs to play for a publisher depending on what they need.

Now it is time to get yourself in the songwriting "scene." This means you hang out where the other songwriters hang out. You support the other songwriters on their performances and you are one of the group as much as you can be—without being annoying, of course. In the scene, as you listen to other songs, you can learn where you stand and more importantly, where your songs stand in the grand scheme of things—if you can be honest with yourself. Are the other writers blowing you away? Are you right in there with them with your songs? Do any of them have publishing deals? These are all things to find out about as you navigate the songwriter scene. Of course, the "scene" has more scenery in the recording centers of the U.S.—Nashville, Los Angeles, and New York, so it might be a good idea to at least visit one or more of those cities while you are getting your songwriting act together.

At some point, you are going to have to have demo recordings of your songs—these must be the best they can be. There is no such thing as poor-quality demo recordings any longer—the quality should be as close to a professional recording released on a label as possible. Again, you must use your good judgment. Since demos are the vehicle your songs will use to get heard, it becomes vital that the recordings are up to snuff. There are a number of ways to go about this process from purchasing your own home studio system to renting a studio and hiring players. Remember all of your songwriting friends you met while hanging out in the scene? Those same people might be able to help you make a great recording, too. I am assuming of course that you also are able to sing your own songs. If singing is the least bit of a problem for you, you MUST get a good vocalist to sing your songs on the demo.

Finally when you believe you are ready, it is time to see a few people. First it is a good idea to meet with one of the artist reps at your PRO. They can listen to your work and give you an idea on where to go or even help you make an appointment or two. You might also make an appointment with an entertainment attorney. Attorneys have valuable insight into the publishing business because they work out publishing deals for writers all the time. Then it becomes time to make appointments with publishers. Make sure you play them your very best and be ready to hear "no thanks," or "the industry is in sad shape right now," and many other ways to hear that they are not interested. Now here is the difficult part ... you stay with it. Keep plugging away in the songwriter scene, keep playing those singer/songwriter nights, and most of all, keep writing songs and making good quality demo recordings. It becomes a matter of "rinse and repeat." With patience and luck, as well as a dose of being at the right place at the right time with the right song, you have just as much of a shot as anyone else.

In New York, an organization called SPONY (Songwriter's Pitch-a-thon of New York) holds an event every month where songwriters play their best song for a panel of three professionals looking for songs. Usually, the panel is made up of publishers and other industry execs. Every song that enters (there is a song maximum) is played for the panel. The panel gives everyone their best listen and usually asks for demos of a few of the songs that catch their interest. This is the kind of activity you should be involving yourself with as you are trying for your publishing deal. Most of all, the best advice you can get is to keep writing and working on your craft, and hopefully something good will come of it.

CHAPTER 10
Yesterday, Today, and What the Future Holds

If you're a musician, a recording engineer, an aspiring record producer, or one of the dozens of individuals who work in the music industry today, I would venture to guess that the majority of days when you wake up and read the music-industry trades, your heart skips a beat, you periodically get short of breath, and then you come to the great realization of "why in the world did I get into this industry?"

I'll tell you why ... It's what we love to do, and there's no other job on this planet that can emulate the excitement, stimulate creativity, and just plain give us that buzz than this industry. However, I'd like to discuss something else that should be very important to all involved in the music industry. We must, let me repeat that, we must not allow what preceded us and what is currently happening in the music industry to sway us in any fashion when it comes to accurately ascertaining what we need to do as musicians and business people as we participate in this industry. All you have to do is get on any music site on the Internet and read that all of the Majors, the Indies, and even the privately owned boutique record companies are panicking in respect to what is going to happen in the music industry in the near future. I would venture to guess this is why no one has made the move toward a new direction that will lead the music industry into a bright new future. When I think of what occurred less than 12 to 15 years ago with Shawn Fanning and Napster. ... Subjectively speaking, if the Majors and the RIAA didn't have the aggressive nature of wanting to keep control of all the intellectual property and therefore the money, the industry would be a totally different entity today. I strongly recommend that all of you look this transaction up in books, articles, periodicals, blogs, and anything else that will enlighten you about this topic.

Therefore, what I'd like us to do in this chapter is to figure out where the music industry has been, and where it is today. However, I think together we should try to manufacture a hypothesis as to what direction "we think" the music industry will be heading in the very near future.

I would like to give special kudos to Alex Cosper for his research on the history of record labels and music industry, and Internet article <http://scribd.com/doc/4067086/A-Brief-History-of-the-Pre-Internet-Music-Business> that was very insightful. Based on that information, I'd like to share the words of Alex Cosper in relation to specific decades that dramatically affected the industry, and then we will break off and I will add my own interpretation/conceptions, as well as those of music-industry professionals.

When you look at music history, particularly within the professional performance realm of commercially successful music, you can assess that technology drives music, and not the other way around. I can recount musical groups throughout music history, particularly beginning in the 1960s, wherein they would incorporate technology within the recording studio … technology that wasn't readily available to the majority of musicians touring at that time. For example, Brian Wilson of the Beach Boys and his use of a variety of unique production techniques gleaned from masters such as Phil Spector and more, and also his use of uncommon musical instruments such as the Theremin, accordion, and other instruments that weren't normally used within the pop/rock genre. Probably the most famous and successful band of all music, the Beatles, which incorporated a plethora of unusual instruments from the sitar and Theremin to many other musical instruments found in countries other than the UK or the United States. One could go as far as to say that much of the credit goes to their phenomenal producer Sir George Martin, whose knowledge of orchestral instrumentation as well as the orchestral repertoire played an integral and important role in the ever-growing sound that the Beatles recordings displayed in a short period of seven years.

As we venture back in time, we find Thomas Edison, who is considered the founder of the modern electrical world. Not only was he the founder of General Electric, which went on to become one of the biggest corporations of all time, but also his developments paved the way for the motion picture and music industries. Some of the many inventions that came out of his team of inventors included the light bulb, the movie camera, and the first audio recording device called the "talking machine." The talking machine first appeared in 1877 as an expansion of the telephone concept, which had been introduced a year earlier by Alexander Graham Bell. Edison's original concept of a recording device was essentially an answering machine to record telephone calls, according to Alex Cosper's research. Dick Weissman, in his book entitled *The Music Business* states that Charles Cros in France came up with a similar idea concerning the phonograph, independent of Thomas Edison, in 1877.

Emile Berliner emerged as Edison's technological competitor in the 1880s. The Columbia Phonograph Company became a third player in 1889, selling dictating machines, under the leadership of Edward Easton. It was originally the American Graphophone Company, set up by telephone inventor Bell, his cousin Chichester Bell, and Charles Tainter. When the company was incorporated in the District of Columbia, it began to take on the name Columbia.

By the 1890s, each major U.S. city had its own phonograph company. Edison established the Edison Speaking Phonograph Company in 1878, then the National Phonograph Company in 1896. Berliner established the American Gramophone Company in 1891 and the United States Gramophone Company in 1893. The Columbia Graphophone Company was the first to go international by setting up offices in London and Paris in 1899.

As you can ascertain from the following information, technology was about to radically change the lives of Americans and all others across the world. I'll cite this again later on in the text; however, it should be noted that generally speaking, technology drives music, the recording of the music, the mastering of the music, the live performance of music, and through the advanced technologies of synthesis, computers, and the like, even the creation of the original song itself could be thought of as being technologically driven. As time moved on, technology grew exponentially. In 1915, Felix Kahn formed the OKed Record Company in the United States, which was also the label that introduced the first blues records. Soon to follow, Emerson Records was formed in 1916, and United Artists was formed in 1919 by early film stars Charlie Chaplin, Douglas Fairbanks, and others, but eventually it crossed into the record business by issuing movie soundtracks. (Cosper)

Through the advent of these new record companies, sales of records moved right along and got as high as almost 1,000,000 in 1927. Then the Great Depression struck, and like every other business in the country, the music industry was hit hard and record sales plummeted to below 40,000 in 1932 (Weismann). An interesting fact should be mentioned here, that even though the recording industry and other industries were bankrupt, two of the thriving businesses during the Great Depression were live music and sales of alcohol. This is an interesting psychological manifestation as we learned that when people were financially struggling and seeking employment, which was very difficult to find, they opted to frequent nightclubs known as the speakeasy. A speakeasy is today's equivalent of a local bar or tavern in which live music is performed. Even though the musicians were barely compensated for performing, just as they we hardly compensated monetarily for performing a manual laborer job, performing live music was still available for those who knew how to play an instrument or sing.

In the 1930s, the Victor Corporation introduced the 78 rpm record and record player. (Cosper) Prior to this time, music was recorded on wax cylinders in which the musician or singer would stand at the large end of a brass horn and sing or play into it. The brass horn, which ranged from one foot to 130 feet in length, was designed to taper down to a device much like a record player's stylus that would then record the performance onto a wax cylinder The record conglomerate known today as EMI, The Electric and Musical Industries, was established in 1931 after the merger of Columbia and the American Gramophone Company. That year EMI opened Abbey Road recording studios in London, England. From the mid- to late 1930s and through the 1940s, the record industry began to grow by leaps and bounds. Record companies such as ARC and Decca were already becoming the two leading record companies of the decade. As I stated before, technology is what drives the industry during the mid-1940s, the company Ampex introduced the reel-to-reel tape recorder on the market. The reel-to-reel tape recorder's primary use prior to the record industry was its ability to record interrogations, which Germany and the U.S. did during World War II. The reel-to-reel tape deck became the

industry standard for recording in the 1940s and 50s. The legendary guitarist, Les Paul, experimented with the reel-to-reel tape deck and came up with a concept of what we call today overdubbing and multi-track recording. What Les Paul would do is record one track into a single reel-to-reel tape recorder, then play back that tape recorder while performing another live track on his guitar that was being recorded by another reel-to-reel tape recorder. This process would be continued until the recording was complete.

Capitol Records became one of the first major record companies on the West Coast around 1942, and was established by recording artist Johnny Mercer. By this time in the music industry, collaborations and mergers between record companies began to evolve. During the late 1940s, the sons of a wealthy Middle Eastern entrepreneur began what is still known today as Atlantic records. Ahmet Ertegun and Herb Abrahamson were some of the first music business pioneers to begin the mega-corporate structure we know today as the record industry. Other record companies that followed in the 1950s were known as the five major record labels of the industry: Columbia, RCA, Decca, Capitol, and Mercury. Capitol Records' clout occurred when the biggest UK record company, EMI, purchased Capitol Records in 1955.

From 1953 to 1955, music that was played on the radio made a dramatic change when pioneering radio disc jockeys such as Alan Freed, Dick Clark, and others began to play R&B recordings by the original songwriters, who at that time were African-American artists. This was the beginning of the change in listenership within the radio industry. No longer did the teenagers listen to the music of their parents, but would tune in to the Alan Freed Moondog radio show to be mesmerized by the sounds and rhythms of what was then known as Rock 'n Roll. The only downfall at this time within the music industry is that the businesspersons with the money did not want African-American artists played on public radio. In order to overcome this presumed pitfall, record companies began to sign white artists, Elvis Presley, Pat Boone, Donovan, Bill Haley and The Comets, and others who were much more palatable to the listening American audience. Elvis Presley and others would perform actual rhythm and blues songs written by African-American artists, who in turn brought these artists' works to the forefront, and before too long they became stars within the Rock 'n Roll industry. Chuck Berry, Little Richard, Bo Diddley, and many others rose to stardom with their original music. Just prior to this period, Leonard and Phil Chess were the proprietors of Aristocrat Records, later renamed Chess Records, which rose to fame by recording the musical greats listed previously.

Television now begins playing an integral role within the music industry. Former DJ Dick Clark launched his famous television show, *American Bandstand*, on the ABC television network. The record industry was on its way! Technologically, the Sony Corporation introduced the first pocket-sized transistor radio in 1957, which allowed listeners to take their music with them wherever they went. In 1958, Warner Bros. Motion Picture Company launched Warner Bros. Records. In the latter part of the 50s, producer Phil Spector, the creator of the Wall of Sound production technique, launched his own company called Spector Records. And finally before the end of the 50s, the great Berry Gordy formed Motown records in Detroit, Michigan, which was solely responsible for some of the greatest artists of the 1960s including Diana Ross and the Supremes, Smokey Robinson, the incomparable Stevie Wonder, and probably the most famous family musical group in the history of recorded music, The Jackson Five, which produced the King of Pop himself ... Michael Jackson.

We need to recognize that many other genres of music were developing concurrently with Rock  'n Roll music. Broadway musicals, Hard Bop, East Coast Jazz, Smooth Jazz of the West Coast, Western Swing and Country-Western music, and many other musical genres were also thriving during this period of the music industry's development. The 1960s brought a great deal of change, not only in music, but also within the music industry as a business. Country and Rhythm & Blues were being recorded at Stax Records in Memphis; Miles Davis, John Coltrane, Thelonious Monk, and other jazz greats were making their mark as well. However, no other group in the history of music had made such a phenomenal impact on both the industry and music itself as The Beatles. It's hard to believe that several American record companies turned down the Beatles when they first came to America searching for a record contract. Executives at several record companies were cited stating,

"The groups with electric guitars were dying and that wasn't the sound they were looking for any more." I would imagine that those executives affiliated with those record companies that turned down the Beatles are still flogging themselves today for that enormous, unrecoverable mistake in judgment! Also during this period, the consolidation of the major record companies began. Warner acquired Reprise Records in 1963, Atlantic Records in 1967, and Electra in 1968. Through other consolidations and music business transactions, the entertainment group Warner Communications was formed.

A huge number of music business transactions and mergers occurred in the 60s. What we need to remember is that by the end of this period the top major labels were CBS, Warner Bros., RCA, Capitol-EMI, PolyGram, and MCA.

Let's forget about the business aspect for the 60s for a moment and think about what happened musically. The music of the 1960s was one of experimentation, new sounds, and new arranging and production techniques. The Beatles and The Beach Boys were probably the two leading groups in music during the 1960s to experiment with different production techniques, instrumentation, and studio performance. Both groups experimented with new instrumentation from the sitar, which originated in India to the Theremin, which was an instrument commonly used in electroacoustic composition. New production techniques introduced by Sir George Martin, Brian Wilson, and others took the production techniques of Phil Spector and brought them to new heights. New sociological developments were made within Rock 'n Roll, now known simply as Rock. The early- to mid-1960s was possibly the first of only two periods wherein music actually influenced society. The introduction of The Beatles to the United States ushered in a new look for Americans via new hairstyles and clothing styles. The Rolling Stones were highly influential by introducing what would be called the Bad Boy look. During this time in England, there were two socioeconomic groups known as the Mods and the Rockers. The Rolling Stones portrayed the rockers, and toward the end of the 1960s the musical group The Who portrayed the Mods look. Of course, there were dozens of Rock, Pop, Country Western, and other music genres during this period. However, the goal of this chapter is not to dissect each decade, but to give you the highlights of what was happening musically and discuss the music business structure itself.

The 1970s began with some changes within the music business structure. WEA was formed in 1970 by the joining of three record labels Warner, Electra, and Atlantic, and would create a mega-distribution operation. With the success of such artists as the Eagles and Jackson Browne, the heads of Atlantic Records formed Asylum records in 1971. Warner Communications bought Asylum, which merged with Electra in 1973, and was kept under the guidance of one of the greatest music-industry businesspersons of all times, David Geffen. The 1970s introduced a brand new genre of music that was highly influenced by the African-American culture. Groups such as Kool and The Gang; Earth, Wind and Fire; Sly and The Family Stone; and solo artists such as Aretha Franklin, Marvin Gaye, Al Green, and many, many others were at the forefront of the music industry. Leading the pack was the great Stevie Wonder. On the Rock side of the musical genre, we had Led Zeppelin, Pink Floyd, David Bowie, Deep Purple, and many others. In 1974, Sugar Hill Records, which was set up by Joe and Sylvia Robinson, issued what can arguably be the first Rap song, "Rapper's Delight" by the Sugar Hill Gang. However, during all this new and inventive music, a new genre of music was being created in which the band or the musical act was not the center of attention, but the audience and/or the dancers in the club were. Here comes Disco Music! The record company RSO went on to become a top disco label of the late 70s, which highlighted the successes of groups such as the Bee Gees, Donna Summer, The Village People, and many others. The Bee Gees and the movie soundtrack *Saturday Night Fever* became the best-selling album in the history of recorded music until Michael Jackson's *Thriller* in

1983 on Epic Records. Before the end of the 70s, a dramatic change within the music industry would occur. An artist by the name of Peter Frampton released an album entitled *Frampton Comes Alive* and took the music industry by storm. Music-industry businesspersons could not comprehend how a solo artist could fill a stadium with people eager to see them perform. Several of the major record conglomerate CEOs and other high-profile businesspersons within the music industry sought to create, I should say re-create, this phenomenon. By the beginning of the 1980s, the music business saw the advent of what we know today as Corporate Rock Bands, or cookie-cutter bands. Musical acts had to have close to the same look, close to the same sound, etc., if they wanted any chance to acquire a record contract. Now this is not to demean nor disparage the list of acts that are to follow, but they do fall into this Corporate Rock category. Journey, Foreigner, Boston, and others fell into this corporate rock mold. This was also a great time for a new style of music to begin that was created in the streets of Queens and Los Angeles. Rick Rubin and Russell Simmons set up Def Jam Records in 1984. The group Run-DMC became the first successful act for that label, as well as LL Cool J, Exit 13, and others. On the other side of the country, Death Row Records was coming into its own with Above the Law, Dr. Dre, NWA, Snoop Dogg, and others. Rap was no longer an underground musical movement—it was permeating the airwaves with its indigenous street life set to complex rhythms and lyrics.

Even while this was happening, a new underground music scene was developing in the Pacific Northwest, known as Grunge. Grunge music is sometimes referred to as the Seattle sound. Its underground groups included Mud Honey, Pearl Jam, Smashing Pumpkins, Mother Love Bone, Soundgarden, and of course the most famous of all ... Nirvana. Music had come full circle. No longer were bands going to dress up like each other and sound like each other, they were going to be individuals. With unique sounds that would appeal to this country's new teen generation.

With the exception of the group Nirvana, the biggest stars of the 1980s were without exception Madonna, Michael Jackson, and Nirvana. By the end of the 1980s, the top major labels were Sony, Warner, PolyGram, BMG, EMI, and MCA.

Provided below is an example of the chronology of record labels from 1925 to a predicted 2015 scenario. This will provide you an example of not only the timeline, but also the major players within the industry during certain decades.

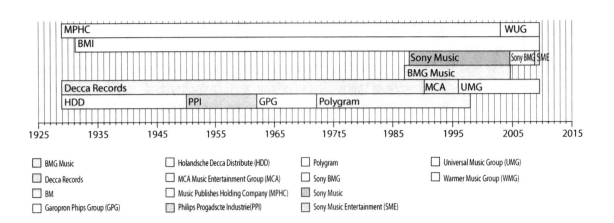

A CHRONOLOGY OF THE MUSIC INDUSTRY RECORD LABELS:

What can be said about the music above the 1990s in the industry itself? Acquisitions of record companies via takeovers are happening almost biannually. In 1990, MCA was bought by Matsushita of Japan, Interscope Records was launched in 1990, and technologically the most important advancement was the usurping of the cassette by the CD. Even though the cassette had 55% of the market compared to 31% for compact discs, it was just a matter of time before the CD would take its place. We see this happening again in 2011 in that the CD will soon be replaced by what the music industry says is going to be the flash drive. Undoubtedly, the technology that would change the music industry, the film industry, the television industry, and life on this Earth in general was the World Wide Web, circa 1989–1990. New technologies had to be developed in order to accommodate this new technology. MPEG (The Motion Picture Experts Group) developed the MP3 as the new medium of storage for computer audio files. As we've discovered, this technology was great in its time, but the audiophile/proactive listener in today's market demands a higher quality sound from its audio.

New businesses and corporations began to develop as more and more companies and the general worldwide public incorporate the Web in their everyday lives. Not only were we affected technologically, but we were also affected legally because of the new laws that needed to be written to address the digital domain of intellectual property. Even though this was initially addressed with compact discs, the availability of an MP3 file delivered by a digital signal through an IP was at an all-time high. The delivery of intellectual property via the digital domain was new, not only to the music industry, but to music-industry legal teams as well. New laws needed to be developed by the United States Copyright Office and Trademark Office to protect the digital intellectual property of its owners. In the late 90s, President Clinton signed the Digital Millennium Copyright Act, which addressed the protection of the intellectual property of the musicians writing the music and more. However, before this began we need to talk about the creation of Shawn Fanning's Napster, a free online service providing access to musical and moving picture digital intellectual property. We are not going to go into the legal mire that Napster created and was soon emulated by many others around the world. The RIAA, known as the Recording Industry Association of America, started a subsidiary group called SoundExchange. This group's sole purpose is to track downloads of digital music around the world. We shouldn't get into a discussion of whether music should be available to the public for free or not at this time. However, copyright law does state that the use of copyrighted intellectual property without the consent of the owner is illegal; therefore, downloading digital music without the consent of its owner is illegal. The creation of Napster and other entities like it put the music industry in disarray. The industry truly did not know how to handle this new development within its realm. Moreover, as we all know, change is difficult ... but for the record industry, this change was impossible and unforgivable. A meeting of all the CEOs of the major record conglomerates, their attorneys, Shawn Fanning, and his attorneys arranged a private meeting to try to come to some solution concerning this dilemma. There are many online and hardcopy resources that you may access that discuss this actual meeting. Needless to say, the Major record conglomerates wanted to shut Napster down ... which in hindsight, was their downfall. The Major record companies are in a state of flux/instability as we speak. Had they listened to reason during these private meetings, they all most likely would have made billions upon billions of dollars! But, as I stated, change is hard.

Acquisitions and reforming of the major conglomerates occurred again. Sony and BMG merged to become Sony/BMG. The other record conglomerates are Warner Music Group, Universal, and possibly EMI ... that's if Guy Hands hasn't single-handedly destroyed the record company when he filed for bankruptcy. Another major music entertainment activity that occurred in the 2000s is when the former New York Attorney General Eliot Spitzer decided to go after the music industry for cases that involved payola. Payola, also known as Pay for Play, is someone (the record company) paying someone else (the radio MD, PD, or DJ) to play an artist's music on the radio.

Probably the greatest success of the 2000s in relation to an artist's development and promotion in music was the creation of the television show *American Idol*. If you were to sit down and analyze this program carefully, you would discover that this is a course in artist development being broadcast all over the world for you to watch and learn how to take an artist from being an unknown and make them into a superstar! This not only gave new musicians the opportunity to gain tremendous exposure via television, but also rekindled the careers of many known artists who have appeared on the show as guest performers. When Steven Tyler from Aerosmith agreed to be a judge, sales of Aerosmith's albums rose nearly 300%! Now that's what I call great marketing.

Because of the unstable nature of the Majors, the Indies have stepped from a historic identity of being a niche market into a place of authority within the music industry. In 2009, for the first time in history, more Grammy Awards went to Independent artists than to Major label artists. How do I translate all this ... I'm not sure I'd be the first one to go out and start a major label, but there's never been a better time for a new act to break into the industry. Record labels are stepping away from the major conglomerate paradigm and becoming—what is now called in L.A.—boutique record companies that will cater to possibly a maximum of 10 artists. Does this sound familiar to anyone? Sounds like an Indie label to me.

When we look around at the development of technology in 2011 and on, it's safe to say that the projected leader in the dissemination of recorded music within the digital medium will most likely be the Apple Corporation via iTunes, and iCloud. All technology periodicals, Websites, blogs, and the variety of musician magazines all point to this fact. However, it will be interesting to watch the development of Facebook and MySpace as they attempt to create an all-in-one stop for your digital entertainment needs. I'm certain we'll all be watching with anticipation ... I know I will be.

RESOURCES:

MtAltra
AllAccess.com
Album Network
Radio & Records
Yahoo.com/Associated Press articles
Video: *The Edison Effect: The Phonograph*, A&E Television Networks/History Channel, AAE-40051, 1995.
America on Record: A History of Recorded Sound by Andre Millard, Cambridge University Press, 1995.
The A-Z Book of Record Labels by Brian Southall, Sanctuary Publishing Ltd, Sanctuary House, London, 2000.
Music Man: Ahmet Ertegun, Atlantic Records, and the Triumph of Rock 'n Roll by Dorothy Jade and Justine Picardie, WW Norton and Co, New York, 1990.
Joel Whitburn's Pop Memories 1890–1954: The History of American Popular Music by Joel Whitburn, Record Research Inc., Menomonee Falls, WI, 1986.
The Fabulous Phonograph: 1877 to 1977 by Roland Gelatt.
Music Business by Dick Weissman, Crown Trade Paperbacks, New York, 1990.

CHAPTER 11
Career Opportunities Within the Music Industry

The big question always is ..."can I get a job and a career in the music industry?"... The answer is ..."yes, you can. ..." The real question then becomes, "what are you willing to DO to have a career in the music industry?" The correct answer here should be "anything and everything." Most of all, people who have talent and the ability to persevere get the gigs.

Internships can be very important because they allow for bottom-level entry into most music-related careers. Internships can be sponsored by a college/university, where the student receives real-world experience in addition to earning academic credits. You can also do an internship on your own without being associated with a university, depending on the type of career and the sponsoring company. Most internships involve the intern working for free; however, there are some that pay. Ideally, the internship would lead to a permanent job after the intern has shown his or her worth. The trick is to find an internship with a company that has the ability to hire you when the time comes, and at the same time, you show the company that they are better off by having you as an employee. The idea of working for free in a place away from home can be daunting—you have all the normal bills to pay during this time such as food, rent, and utilities—but this is usually the way in. Some careers do not have a way in via internships (songwriting, for example). These careers require graduation from the school of experience, paying dues, and real-life hard knocks.

The following is a partial listing of careers in the music industry with a short description of each, and an idea of how to get into the job. This is by no means a complete listing, but, it should cover most of the bases. For purposes of this book, we will limit descriptions to jobs directly related to music.

CAREERS IN MUSIC COMPOSITION/SONGWRITING/PERFORMING

Songwriter

Today's songwriter has two important tasks, the first of which is to write great songs. The craft of songwriting sometimes takes a long time to develop, yet for some, the craft comes perfectly naturally. The next important task comes after the song is written, which is to do something with the song, namely get other artists to "cut" (record) the song. This part requires a lot of determination and patience, as well as a willingness to constantly work the songs. The songwriter should be in the songwriter scene at all times to let song users know they are out there and constantly writing. If things go well, the songwriter will be signed by a publisher usually for a one-year term, and in that term the publisher and songwriter work together to get the songs first accepted by the publishing company, and then cut by the biggest artist willing to put the song on their recording. The professional songwriting career is all about writing songs that other artists will use through a publisher, not necessarily for the songwriter to perform. Being able to play your own songs, however, can go a long way when trying to sell someone on your song.

Composer

The composer differs from a songwriter in that he or she creates works that are more serious in nature (think orchestral score as opposed to songs). The composer also works in various genres that require incidental music. Although such writing could be a song (enter the songwriter), the composer is more about writing using various instruments or electronic sounds or both. Composers typically have studied music, arranging, and counterpoint at a university and can deliver music in a broad range of genres. Music for video and film requires the composer to write in support of the action on the screen. This can be a sweeping orchestral score or an avant garde piece, depending on what the director wants to hear. Not to be overlooked is composing for multimedia or video games. Many have a large budget associated with the game's score, and this can require a specific kind of composing where one theme might easily transition into many others depending on where the player is in the game. Yet another avenue for composing is music for advertising, which will many times rely on a specific very memorable theme and be only 30 seconds to one minute long. You can probably think of a few themes lodged in your head for particular products or services. The composer in all of these idioms will more often than not work under extreme time constraints and he or she must deliver or risk the next job from that particular client and others, if negative word of mouth runs rampant. Just as with songwriters, composers have to do the groundwork of constantly being in the composer scene and reminding users they are out there ready to work.

Performer

Singers can find work as background vocalists and production singers (singers brought in on recordings) as well as soloists and recording artists. Some singers combine their talent with songwriting, which makes them a double threat in terms of employment (a singer-songwriter). For the most part, singers have an idea of whether or not they can get an audience to respond early on, either in school/ university or in semi-professional and amateur-level local clubs. Singers make their living singing on recordings or in live performance, so the singer should find a good manager early in their career in order to position themselves to get bigger and better gigs, as well as recording contracts. It should be mentioned that there are singers who have a good career going who are not great singers ... they get by on personality, charisma, and perhaps acting ability. This is the exception, however; usually the one requirement for a singer is to be able to sing, and sing very well. Some singers will give students singing lessons when they are not touring or recording in order to make money between gigs.

Instrumentalists also get work on recordings, live performances, and teaching. Like singers, the main requirement for instrumentalists is to be accomplished on the instrument—something that usually starts as a child and then continues and grows throughout their career. For in-studio work, musicians should be able to sight read exceptionally well, which means that a musician can correctly play a piece of music from the moment they see it without any practicing whatsoever. Studio work also requires the musician to be familiar with and capable of playing a variety of genres: whatever comes up they should be able to play it and play it well. Live performance requires a slightly different skill set, as in the ability to play nearly perfectly for every night of the show, not to mention the ability to travel well (and keep healthy—away from all of the junk food!). Auditions are a normal part of the live-performance musician's life, and are, of course, taken very seriously. For many commercial music acts, the audition requirement is to simply "learn the songs from the CD;" therefore, the musician should be able to learn all parts by ear while listening to the recording. A musician's work tends to ebb and flow; during the lean times, the musician might engage in a part-time job or music-related job in songwriting, management, teaching, or some of the other career options available to them.

CAREERS IN MUSIC PRODUCTION

Arranger

An arranger takes existing music or a song, and creates "parts" for different instruments to play. An arranger also might take a larger score and create a piano reduction for a solo piano. Either way, an arranger earns their money by being very adept (and fast) at arranging a piece of given music. Most arrangers work on a freelance basis for performers, writing custom arrangements for a particular artist's show. Nearly every arranger is also adept at composing because of the similar educational background involved. Professional arrangers excel at music theory, composition, counterpoint, and ear training. Starting out, arrangers try to get as much experience as they can, writing arrangements (many times for free) and revising their arrangements after hearing them in a rehearsal setting. After a lot of trial and error, and after enough repetitions of the same process, an arranger becomes more viable. As with any other field, top arrangers are always in demand, while the upstart arrangers have ground to cover before making a career out of it.

Copyist

The copyist creates individual scores from a given arrangement. Generally, copyists are themselves strong in music theory and arranging. Copyists should be familiar with notation software such as Finale or Sibelius in order to create publisher-ready scores. Many copyists are also composers and arrangers starting out their careers or filling in with work between arranging jobs.

Conductor

The conductor leads a group, ensemble, orchestra, or band, directing them during performances. The conductor spends much time preparing to conduct by studying scores and rehearsing the group, preparing for performances. The conductor works with arts administrators to help manage the business and artistic affairs of the orchestra or group. Many times the conductor is responsible for administrative tasks such as planning a musical season for an orchestra and hiring of musicians for the ensemble. There are many ensemble types that require the use of a conductor, from opera and ballet companies to musical theater and full-on orchestras. Many conductors have assistant conductors to take care of some of the rehearsals. The assistant conductor is the entry-level point for this kind of job. Most conductors are extremely familiar with symphonic music through years of study at the university level.

Editor

The editor works for a print music company and is responsible for the production of print music for a variety of ensembles as well as simplified piano/vocal arrangements. Editors should be expert with notation software and pre-press techniques. Editors also serve to proofread submissions from outside arrangers and essentially are responsible for the print company's product lines. Typically editors have studied music composition and music theory, much like composers and arrangers, with the added experience of print publication and preparing scores and content for the printing press.

Music Director

The job title "music director" can mean a number of things. One would be a symphony conductor (discussed under "conductor"). Another type of music director might be someone who performs in a band or group, is given responsibility to hire and fire other group musicians, and takes care of any musical arrangements involving the group. Many times this will be someone whom an artist trusts completely. Similarly, there are a number of churches both large and small that have music directors leading other musicians in the church group. A music director might also be someone who has contracted to compose and arrange for a particular TV show or movie, and then is expected to direct the performing ensemble.

Music Producer

The producer is involved with creating music that satisfies both the artist and the label (or whoever is funding the project). An entire chapter is devoted to producers earlier in this book. Typically, the producer is the person who finds the best songs for the artist to record, and then coordinates the process of recording the song. Various types of producers stem from the various experiences a producer might bring to the table. One producer might be a great vocal coach, another might be an excellent instrumentalist, and still another might be very good at raising money for a project and calling upon others to put everything together. A producer's success or failure comes in the form of hit records or market flops—the more hits, the greater the demand for the producer's talents. Just as in other freelance-style careers in the music industry, the producer's work tends to be from job to job. For this reason, the producer tends to have a number of projects going at the same time, or to be involved in other aspects of the music industry such as management, songwriting, publishing, and concert promotion. The producer is also responsible for staying within a budget for the recording. Usually, a producer has had previous successes in some other aspect of music industry before an artist and a label will trust and rely upon them. Leadership ability is also important—the producer should be able to communicate effectively with all of the persons involved in making a recording, especially the artist and the recording engineer.

Recording Engineer

The recording engineer has the responsibility of making the vision of the artist and producer come to life from a technical standpoint. The engineer should be completely familiar with all studio equipment (console, microphones, signal processing, etc.) so that the best possible and most appropriate recording can be made. Such equipment can be extremely complex, but the engineer must be able to navigate quickly and according to the pace of the session at hand. Most engineers start on the ground floor as interns, assistants, or in client services (in other words, a gopher and bathroom cleaner). Those who stick with it find their way to assisting on bigger and bigger projects, and finally move up to engineer. Staff engineers are employed by a studio facility and will "come with" the studio as part of the studio fee. Independent engineers, like independent producers, go from job to job, hopefully with a string of hits behind them. The engineer who was responsible for the latest hit sound will be in high demand by producers and artists. There are number of colleges, universities, and trade schools that train students in the art and science of making recordings. Such students upon graduation soon find that they must also serve as an intern before landing a coveted staff engineer position. Their education comes into play when they are faced with their first pressurized "for-real" session, then hopefully the years spent learning about the recording arts will come to bear. A particular engineer might have a background in electronics or physics, and others might have a music background. In either case ,both have to do the job at hand without losing sight of the bigger picture, which is always getting the best and most appropriate sound for the artist and producer.

Mastering Engineer

The mastering engineer's studio is the last stop of a music recording before it goes out to the masses. The mastering engineer will typically have an extremely good listening environment that represents the best in quality. The mastering engineer's job is to tweak the final mix coming from the producer, artist, and recording engineer. Such tweaking might include adding equalization, compression (to make the mix seem louder), and very specialized signal processing designed for this purpose. Until the next technology replaces it, the mastering engineer might also make the best quality MP3 files of all the songs as well. The mastering engineer also locks in the song order for CDs and prepares a CD for the duplication plant. Mastering requires a very special set of "ears" to be effective, ears that know where a mix is, and how much tweaking is necessary for public consumption. A mastering studio might have internships available for entry into the business, or the engineer might be willing to take on an apprentice who shows great promise.

Live-Sound Engineer

The live-sound engineer is responsible for sound reinforcement of concerts using equipment specialized for this purpose. Good live-sound engineers are always in demand for tours and concerts; however, it is one of those things where good ones who stick with it are sometimes difficult to pin down because of the high demand for their services. Concert sound companies responsible for supplying concert sound systems are good places to start this kind of career, but it is the freelance, large tour engineer who commands serious money. Like other engineering types of work, freelance live-sound engineers tend to go from job to job (rather than a salaried position). One can usually find a position as an audio tech on a concert tour, which is another ground-level entry point. The audio tech would be responsible for the "dirty work" of plugging in cables, heavy lifting, etc. There is also demand for such engineers with companies that do event services—which involves the set-up and operation of smaller sound systems for conferences and meetings in hotels and convention centers. Such jobs may or may not directly involve music.

Audio Maintenance Engineer

The audio maintenance engineer is in one of the most needed occupations as far as recording studio work is concerned. This person knows how to troubleshoot and fix audio equipment that breaks down in recording studios. Nowadays recording engineers tend to come from a recording "arts" background rather than from an E.E. background (electrical engineering) and they are unable to troubleshoot and fix today's very complex audio equipment. Good audio maintenance engineers are always busy in the recording centers of the country (New York, Nashville, Los Angeles). Many such engineers are involved in the design and modification of audio equipment, for which studios are willing to pay to have custom-designed gear. Good audio maintenance engineers should understand both analog and digital audio electronics, and if they are effective, keep up with new gear, and expertly restore analog gear, they should have a long career doing this kind of work. Equipment in studios always needs maintenance at some point, and this is great job security for the maintenance engineer. In between jobs, the audio maintenance engineer might work for audio equipment dealers, modifying and fixing gear for them as well as for project studios.

Music for Video/ Film/Multimedia/Sound Designer

Since the outbreak of cable television and hundreds of channels per household, the need for video content is ever increasing, which in turn creates an increasing need for music to go along with the video. Films, television, and video games with both large and small budgets need musical content. The main idea is to produce music that enhances and supports what is happening on the television, film, or computer screen. Audio engineers working with video, film, and multimedia have a hand in music production, and mixing music (much like the music-only engineer), as well as placing music in a film or video soundtrack. Additionally, such engineers also work with dialog production and sound effects, which is in the realm of the sound designer. In large-budget feature films, music, dialog, and sound effects are mixed together at the same time on mega-recording consoles all while watching the film on the large screen, and usually under intense deadline pressure. This kind of work is also known as audio post-production, meaning that music, dialog, and sound effects are already produced and then put into place after the fact. Careers in audio post-production generally begin the same way as audio engineers—with internships and apprenticeships that hopefully then lead to a permanent position.

Instrument Designer/Manufacturer/Repair

Musical instruments are omnipresent from the hobbyist to the professional. Instruments must be designed and built by hand or in a factory. Custom or master instrument builders are few, but many of them can take on an apprentice who shows promise. Some designers are traditionally based and have been building the same instruments based on hundreds of years of refinement—violin makers, for example. Other designers find new ways to make and manufacture their instruments in order to keep costs down and maintain quality. Some companies that manufacture instruments are international conglomerates and usually always have job openings, especially in sales for the go-getter hustler types. Instrument repair and maintenance is something always needed, and is also accessible from the journeyman/apprenticeship angle, since there are very few programs in community colleges and higher education that offer courses in instrument building and repair.

CAREERS IN MUSIC RADIO BROADCASTING

Disk Jockey

The disk jockey at a radio station is responsible for announcing songs, filling up airtime between songs with commentary, and most importantly, reading advertisement copy (scripts). Popular DJs who rise in the ranks high enough to be able to pick and choose songs to play on air become a target for record labels' marketing arms to influence. DJs are routinely encouraged to function as announcers and commentators for special promotional events as well as introducing acts at live concerts. DJs also tend to be responsible for creating on-air ads and public service announcements (PSAs) in the radio station's production studio. A college education in broadcasting is not required for DJ jobs, but it can help to get practical experience in a college radio station. Such experience and a reel of examples of the DJ on air are valuable in finding a job. DJs must be able to read copy flawlessly and without sounding like they are reading, and generally have a personable attitude.

Program Director

The program director (PD) is responsible for putting shows together and producing for a radio station, including the responsibility for picking songs to air as well as creating the schedule for on-air personalities. PDs can also be responsible for hiring and firing of DJs. In most radio stations, the PD will have multiple roles—sometimes as a DJ, selling advertising, and organizing special events. Program directors are often the target of label radio-promotion personnel who try to get them to play songs from their catalog of music, especially in major markets in big cities.

CAREERS IN MUSIC MANAGEMENT

Talent Agent

The talent agent is responsible for procuring work for the artist. Talent agents therefore have to be in contact with those who purchase talent, as well as performers and their personal managers. Agents try to find the balance between how much money a buyer can pay versus how much an artist can get. Agents and agencies take a commission from the work they procure, usually 10%–15%. Large agencies (such as ICM and CAA) may have more entry-level positions available than smaller local agencies who run a two- or three-person operation, although a student might get more experience out of an internship at a smaller agency.

Arts Administrator

The arts administrator is responsible for management of a non-profit classical music symphony or group. This type of manager has the task of working within a budget that comes from donors and other outside sources, rather than any profit the group can produce (which usually is none). Typically the arts administrator wears a number of hats at once, such as working with the artistic director on programming, with the press on public relations, and with the symphony or group on contracts and concert needs. There are a number of schools around the country that offer master's degrees in arts administration, and such degrees plus practical experience (through an internship of some type) are the way through the employment door.

Concert Promoter

The concert promoter's job is to buy talent from a talent agent, rent a concert venue, put on the concert, and try to make profit from this activity. In many cases, the concert promoter works with co-sponsors such as corporations, local radio stations, and the artists' record label in order to underwrite (raise money for) the concert. Budget preparation is of great importance to the concert promoter, where simple mistakes, overlooking expensive details, and undue optimism about the event can cost big money. Promoters are responsible for the entire event and must make consideration for a variety of items related to artists and concerts, from contracting for sound and lighting services to venue security. Other functions occur as needed: Advertisement, catering, liability insurance, and so on. Concert promoters will usually have openings for interns, especially interns who are the energetic go-getter type.

Personal Manager

An artist engages with a personal manager for one primary purpose: To further the artist's career. At first, the primary goal is to get an artist a recording contract. Once established, the manager then begins to put together the artist's team consisting of an agent/agency, business manager, road manager, publishing company, and publicist. The personal manager becomes the point person in every aspect of the artist's career. Personal managers work on commission ranging anywhere from 10% to 20% for a period of 1 to 3 years. Good ground-floor entrepreneurial opportunity exists here if one can find an artist who's a diamond in the rough and successfully get them signed to a label deal. Other opportunities are available through interning and working for a personal management company.

Music Publisher

The music publisher collects and administers over copyrighted music. Copyrighted music comes from music composers and songwriters. Music publishers then work to exploit their copyrighted music by getting other artists to record their material, and placing their songs in television, film, and advertisement campaigns. Publishers also work to ensure they are getting all royalties due to them. Music publishers range in size from a small operation requiring that the publisher engage in all aspects of publishing to large multinational conglomerates where members of a publishing department focus on specific tasks.

Song Plugger

Song pluggers work for songwriters, representing their work to music publishers, recording artists, producers, managers, and A&R, all to try to get a publishing deal or have a recording artist record their client's song. Usually song pluggers will have a number of clients each with a number of songs to shop. Song pluggers also work directly for music publishers doing the same type of work: Getting songs to the producers, artists, and other people who use them.

Road Manager

The road manager is responsible for making sure that everything involved with touring goes as smoothly as possible. To be effective, road managers must stay in constant contact with the artist (who is on the road with them), the artist's label, publicist, and talent agent. The road manager must "advance" tour date locations to make sure everything from the artist's technical rider is adhered to and to make sure all the details such as hotel stays, per diem money (funds to cover daily expenses for artists and crew), backstage passes, etc., go according to plan. The road manager is also the chief of the road crew, responsible for show set-up, operation, and tear down, and most importantly responsible for organizing transportation between shows. In many cases, the road manager will also serve as one of the crew (front-of-house sound engineer, monitor engineer, merchandiser, etc.) in order to have fewer people out on the road (and save on expenses). As with all the manager types, a good road manager will be very organized and detail oriented. On larger tours, entry-level positions can be available to assist road managers, keeping in mind that every person on the tour represents an expense and another mouth to feed from the budget.

CAREERS IN MUSIC BUSINESS/MERCHANDISING

Music Merchandising (Sales)

Music merchandising involves selling music products to professional and amateur customers. Categories include keyboard instruments, fretted instruments (guitars and basses), wind instruments, brass instruments, percussion instruments, sound reinforcement equipment, and recording equipment. Sales jobs in this area can be involved with specific product sales, wholesale and distribution where the seller works directly for a manufacturer, or on the floor of a music products retail store. In any case, sales of music merchandise requires the seller to be extremely familiar with the products and their place within the music industry in order to be an effective salesperson. Sellers can work for a commission on what they sell, an hourly rate, or a salary, all depending on the type of job and the company selling the merchandise. Most entry-level positions within the music industry are with music retailers, and this kind of job can be a good fall-back option for professional musicians when they're in between jobs.

Retail Sales Manager

The retail sales manager operates and manages a music retail store. The sales manager possesses business-related skills such as accounting and marketing, which are essential to running a business. The retail sales manager is often required to hire and fire sales force in the store, order and restock products, and coordinate marketing and promotional plans.

Typically a sales manager has worked their way up to the position, starting in the company as a salesperson.

Technical Support

Technical support personnel offer training and telephone-based consulting on a particular music product or music system, usually music technology software or other hardware technology. Typically, technical support staff works for a particular manufacturer and must be extremely knowledgeable about their product, as well as the various problems their users encounter. Tech support personnel often require training on the particular company's products, and in many cases are also involved in sales. Although technical support jobs can be entry-level positions, music technology companies want their support employees to have a broad music technology background, often requiring two- or four-year degrees in the area of study.

Business Manager

Business managers handle finances for musicians, have backgrounds in accounting and finance, and knowledge of the music business and its workings. Many business managers are Certified Public Accountants (CPAs) and are able to offer tax and investment advice to clients. Business managers collect a percentage of their clients' gross income for their services (usually 5%), or they negotiate a flat weekly or monthly fee. Usually by the time an artist needs a business manager, significant and steady money is coming in the door. Personal managers will often work with the artist to find a good business manager.

Music Supervisor

The music supervisor chooses, negotiates, and incorporates pieces of music into film, television, and other media such as video games. They may work within production companies, film companies, or television networks. The music supervisor's primary function is to meet the musical needs of the director, usually under a strict budget—perhaps 5% of the overall budget for the production. Typical placement spots are the opening and end credits, with pieces of music throughout the production that enhance the action on the screen. After getting the budget handed to them, they begin the work of licensing music for the film or creating new music for the film. There is no clear-cut career path to becoming a music supervisor, some have degrees in music, some do not. It is important to have a broad familiarity of music, including popular styles and artists, as well as the production process. Since music supervisors work with contracts between publishers, clearances, and negotiations, a legal background would be a good start. Music supervisors develop relationships with film and television directors, music publishers, and producers to have access to fresh musical content, as well as access to hit songs. Generally music supervisors come with experience in the film or television industry, and have a track record of successful music licensing.

Music Contractor

The music contractor serves as the point person for hiring music groups for recording sessions and live events, acting as an agent for the musicians' union. The contractor may also act as conductor for the engagement. Experience as a performer or instrumentalist is usually the necessary background to act as a music contractor for the AFM.

Music Rights Manager

This career involves tracking and managing royalties collection and disbursements for a music publisher or record label. Usually a background in music publishing and accounting is required. Careers in this field can be found with the industry giants (BMG, Sony, Warner, etc.) or with smaller independent companies. All are interested in maximizing royalty income, and this job can require some tenacity in getting royalty payers to pay. This type of job involves issuing invoices and reviewing statements pertaining to royalty income and outflow.

CAREERS IN RECORD LABEL OPERATIONS

A&R Executive

The A&R coordinator is responsible for finding and signing new talent for the label. The coordinator represents the label at various venues where new artists perform. This person is also tasked with finding songs for artists to perform and record. Constant contact with publishers, attorneys, and other networking opportunities is essential for this position. Success in A&R is measured by the number of hit-making artists the A&R person signs, and this person must have the ability to recognize talent and star potential.

A&R Administrator

A&R administrators are responsible for the clerical function of an A&R department. This includes setting budgets for the label's artists as well as accounting for those budgets. The coordinator is also responsible for negotiating with various music entities (studios, art departments, etc.) in order to find cost savings for the label. People in these positions have usually worked their way up the record-label ladder from entry-level positions.

Publicist

The publicist is responsible for the interface between a label's acts and the press, coordinating record releases with press releases. The publicist's main job is to constantly feed information to the press about the label's artists, informing them of promotional campaigns of established as well as new artists. The publicist arranges for interviews and media appearances for the label's artists and handles special promotional events. Publicists are also responsible for public relations of the label and its artists, and at times are called upon to mitigate negative publicity.

Artist Relations Representative

The artist relations representative is the liaison between the label and the artist, and concerned with the general well-being of the label's investment in the artist. The artist relations rep tries to settle disputes and differences that may arise between artists and the label as well as acts in an advisory role to the artist's team of professionals. As the interface between the artist and label, the artist relations representative coordinates marketing and promotional campaigns with tours and performances by the artist, and stays in constant contact with personal managers of their artists.

Radio Promoter

The radio promoter is primarily responsible for getting songs played on the radio. Staff radio promoters are in constant contact with music and program directors at radio stations and work to bring new artists to the station's attention using promotional materials. Radio promoters have the ability to sell and get radio stations excited about new releases. Often, the radio promoter works closely with the label's marketing and promotional team to coordinate efforts in a particular area, the idea would be to create a "perfect storm" of a media blitz including appearances by the artist.

Marketing

The marketing department is responsible for generating plans and strategies to promote their artists. Marketing campaigns can cover all media, including Web-based media and social networking sites. The marketing department and their budgets are usually what make major labels preferable to independent labels. A background in business and marketing as well as knowledge of the music industry are required for this type of job.

Sales

The record label sales department is responsible for managing sales with the various accounts buying the music of the label. The sales department implements marketing and promotional campaigns with sales locations, as well as tracks sales figures for the various artists on the label. Sales departments will usually have one or more people who work with large accounts such as WalMart and Target, which are industry leaders in retail CD sales.

CAREERS IN MUSIC LEGAL SERVICES

Entertainment Lawyer

This job requires a law degree (JD) and passing the state's bar exam. Entertainment lawyers specialize in intellectual property and copyright. Such attorneys are called upon to negotiate the various contracts involved with the music industry (record deals, publishing, management, etc.). Typically, an entertainment lawyer starts with an established law firm to learn the business and can break out on their own once they become successful and make enough contacts. Entertainment attorneys have access to recording-industry decision makers and can work such contacts to get new artists signed.

Paralegal

The paralegal assists entertainment attorneys in their capacity to research copyrights, analyze contracts, and other duties that under the direct supervision of a lawyer. Paralegals do not have a law degree; rather, they can be employable upon finishing a bachelor's degree in legal studies. In many cases, paralegals are the front lines of attorney's offices, engaging in the primary legal work and research required by the law practice.

CAREERS IN MUSIC EDUCATION

Elementary School Music Teacher

The elementary school music teacher is responsible for implementing the music curriculum designated by school, county, or state boards. Elementary school music teachers concentrate on introducing students in K–6 grades to all aspects of music, sometimes conduct beginning ensembles, and give group music lessons. Most curricula will try to involve all elementary students in musical activity such as singing and playing on rhythmic instruments. Many elementary school teachers can spot talent even at early ages and may recommend that parents give the child private lessons. Elementary school music teachers have at least a four-year music education degree as well as teacher certification in their particular state.

Secondary School Music Teacher

The secondary school music teacher teaches students from grades 7 through 12, often concentrating in a particular area such as choral music, band music, or music reading and instrumental lessons. The budget for secondary school music teachers depends on the commitment and funding for the music programs in the school system. The secondary school music teacher is often an integral part of a child's musical education. Music teachers are responsible for entering their schools' bands and choirs into competitions and for putting on plays and musical productions. Fundraising for the school's ensembles and programs is also a part of the job. Such teachers will have at least a four-year music education degree plus teacher certification in their particular state.

Music Education Supervisor

Music education supervisors are primarily responsible for setting a school system's music curriculum and administering over teachers within their school's programs. The music education supervisor is generally someone who has made a career of secondary school music teaching and typically has a doctoral degree in education. The supervisor stays in contact with his school district's music departments though visiting and meeting with the teachers under his purview.

College/University Music Professor

University professors are hired for their particular expertise in their field of music study, and such jobs provide secure income with benefits. Areas of expertise could be instrumental or vocal music instruction, music theory, composition, music history, or other kinds of music instruction (such as music technology, business, etc.). Generally such professors are accomplished as musicians and educators and are well respected in their field. A doctoral degree is usually required, although, some positions allow for a master's degree plus significant professional experience. University professors must be on top of their respective fields, often required to perform nationally or internationally, or to publish in well-respected academic journals. Music professors go through a tenure process designed to gauge the professor's impact and stature in their field of study. During the tenure process, the professor submits a lengthy dossier and resume to a committee who makes a decision on tenure for the faculty member. If the committee agrees, then the positive recommendation goes up the chain to the dean, academic vice president, and ultimately the president and board of trustees of the university. Upon the granting of tenure, the professor usually gets a rank promotion to associate professor. Trouble arises usually when tenure is not granted—there is almost always an appeal, which may or may not be effective. If tenure is denied, the music professor is given a one-year grace period in order to find another job and must leave after that year. Academic jobs can be found by searching the Chronicle of Higher Education and other sources such as

the College Music Society (CMS) and the Music Educators National Conference (MENC). The standard hiring procedure is the formation of a search committee who takes in all applications, narrows them down to three, and then brings those three candidates to campus for a grueling day of interviews and teaching demonstrations. In most cases, one candidate emerges and is offered the job.

Junior colleges also have music programs, more general in nature. Music faculty in two-year schools focus on more general music courses such as music appreciation and music theory. There are, however, a number of two-year programs specializing in fields such as music instruction, music business, and technology.

Studio Instructor

Private music instructors teach individual instrumental or vocal students, from beginners to advanced professionals. Such instructors can operate their own business or work through a local music retailer. Private music instructors are able to set their own fees and schedule, usually teaching students once per week. Most private instructors are accomplished performers, using their teaching gig to generate regular income. Good instructors are in high demand, often working 40- to 60-hour weeks to serve the needs of all of their students. Private instructors schedule and coordinate recitals for their students to perform. Some music retail or instruction centers will take care of the finances for all of their teachers and pay the instructor by the lesson, taking a percentage of the instructor's fee—usually 25%–33%. Advanced degrees are not required of private studio instructors, only the ability to play and teach well. Instructors teaching out of their homes or in music retailers must set up a strict cancellation policy requiring advance notice. Typically a student will pre-pay for a block of lessons in order to reduce the number of no-shows. Typical fees for lessons are from $35 to $50 per hour. Large cities with their own symphony might produce high-level teachers commanding upward of $100 per hour. Music retailers offering lessons make a large chunk of their business from music instruction, and the students (and their parents) are in their store every week buying supplies and accessories. Much research has been done correlating music skills with math skills, and the confidence-building that music lessons provide is exceptional.

Music Librarian

The music librarian is responsible for the catalog of recorded music, print music and other music-related books, as well as acquisition of those materials. Generally music libraries are associated with colleges and universities or large public libraries. Music librarians typically earn an undergraduate degree in music and then a master's degree in library science. A good music librarian will be knowledgeable in many facets of music and most importantly, know where to find good sources for research. Many maintain digital libraries of downloadable music, and do so in a legal manner, paying appropriate fees to subscription services and other digital-rights management services.

OTHER CAREERS IN MUSIC

Music Therapist

The music therapist combines a study of psychology and music. The music therapist treats children and adult patients with various developmental or psychological disorders using music as a delivery method for treatment. Therapists use techniques such as receptive music listening, music and movement, music with touch therapy, even songwriting and lyric discussion. Therapists help improve or maintain quality of life in various areas (brain functioning, motor skills, behavior, etc.). Music therapists often work with a team of health specialists in designing treatment programs for individuals and groups. Music therapists have master's degrees in their field and must also pass a national board certification test to be eligible to practice.

Music Journalist

The music journalist writes about music and its personalities, and writes reviews on concerts and new music releases. Music journalists are employed by newspapers and magazines, or freelance to various publications. The music journalist should be very familiar with specific genres in order to write from a commanding perspective. Many media outlets receive constant press releases from label publicists and must sort through to find the best story. Often music journalists will be part of an overall entertainment journalism department. Such journalists usually get their start by writing (for free) for small publications and college/university newspapers, then graduate to more prestigious positions within the print world based on their work.

CPSIA information can be obtained at www.ICGtesting.com
Printed in the USA
LVOW091614080113

314879LV00007B/122/P